Other books by Alan Abel

CRAZY ADS

THE GREAT AMERICAN HOAX

YOURS FOR DECENCY

THE BUTTON BOOK

THIS IS A DIRTY, ROTTEN, FILTHY BOOK

THE CONFESSIONS OF
A HOAXER

THE CONFESSIONS OF
A HOAXER

by Alan Abel

The Macmillan Company

Library of Congress Catalog Card Number: 72-90246

First Printing

The Macmillan Company
Collier-Macmillan Canada Ltd., Toronto, Ontario
Printed in the United States of America

TO MY MOTHER,
who made it all possible

ACKNOWLEDGMENTS

My thanks to: Joe Franklin for introducing me to editor Alan Rinzler; my wife, Jeanne, for her corrections, revisions and distractions; Marvin Kitman, who laughed; landlord Stanley Stahl for not raising the rent; the inspiration provided by Rosenblum's lean corned beef sandwiches; the New York Sanitation Department, whose noisy garbagemen kept me awake; Mrs. Rosenberg at the corner cigar store for her encouragement to "hurry up and finish so I can read"; and last but not least, the foresight of the thieves at Long Beach, Long Island, last summer who stole all my belongings but left behind a final draft of this book.

ALAN ABEL

CONTENTS

PREFACE

Alan Abel is a scamp, a rascal, a rogue. While he has supported himself at various times as a comedian, a drummer, an advertising copywriter and a free-lance publicity man, his preoccupation has been hoaxes. He is one of the great jesters of recent times, with an irrepressible flair for comic improvisation.

Abel's satirical spoofs are welcome today because we are exposed to so much ill-conceived and nonpractical joking in real life that is often cruel, harmful and profit motivated. We forget that in the hands of the adept the practical joke can be an art form, neither malicious nor destructive but funny. His hoaxes, like any genuine works of art, need no other justification than their own existence.

Richard P. Frisbie
U.S. CATHOLIC

THE CONFESSIONS OF
A HOAXER

ONE

THE LIFE OF
A HOAXER

Dear Allen Able,

I saw you on the Merv Griffith show last night and I'd like to know what's so indesent about a horses penis. Your crazy to want to put pants on animals. God made them naked. Its all in the Bible.

I'm married with three grown children and when we lived on a farm our kids saw sex since they was six! It never hurt them to see naked pigs make love. Maybe what *you* need is a good healthy hump. You jackass you! Your about the dumbest son of a bitch I ever watch on Tv. Fuck you.

I run a gas station along a highway and I fill up some pretty crazy peoples cars. But you take the cake. If you ever drove in I'd squirt grease all over you and stick the

nozle up your red communist ass. You sure make me
mad enough to write anybody for the first time. Thank
God we don't have your kind around here.

S.G.

Now what had I done to upset S.G. so, besides plead for
good, God-fearing, mother-loving people to cover all nude
animals? This letter was representative of the batch I received after appearing on *The Merv Griffin Show* in
January of 1969 along with Arthur Treacher, John Cassa-
vetes, Tony Randall and Jack Carter. At the request of
Chet Collier, executive producer of the show, I had
launched into a ten-minute monologue decrying the prurient effect of naked animals on small children, urging that
all pets be clothed for the sake of decency—and I ended
with a warning to millions of viewers: "Remember, a
nude horse is a rude horse!"

Randall, Carter and Treacher seemed perplexed by my
tirade, as though wondering if I were a serious nut. Cassa-
vetes leaned toward me during a commercial to say,
"You're an actor, aren't you?" Griffin, who knew I was a
professional hoaxer, never revealed the joke and played it
perfectly straight, even to the point of closing his show
with a comment to the audience: "This guy was weird,
wasn't he?"

Although it has been revealed many times over the past
ten years that this tongue-in-cheek campaign is a hoax—I
even wrote a book about it*—I can capture an entirely
new audience of believers by announcing with a straight
face: "I think every horse should wear Bermuda shorts
and every cow a half-slip."

Here are a few more responses to my fictitious Society

* *The Great American Hoax*, New York, Trident Press, 1966.

for Indecency to Naked Animals (S.I.N.A.), first from the Greater East St. Louis Humane Society:

> The members of our society (all volunteers) constantly receive calls to do something about the dogs in school yards, especially when females are in season. It is most embarrassing to the teachers and children to witness the dogs' actions. We want to pick up these little females and keep them away from the public but we do not have a place wherein to keep them. We are stopped in avoiding this situation until we have a shelter and we are wondering if your organization has any plans for assistance in such a delicate matter.

I replied:

> Our organization has already submitted plans to President Nixon for 100,000 animal comfort stations to be placed strategically in cities throughout the country. Undoubtedly, this is the kind of leadership we can all look forward to.

My "fan" letters continue to average about 150 letters a week. Policemen, prisoners, doctors, lawyers, psychologists (even congressmen!) and ordinary people express their hostilities toward my attempts to fiddle with their funny bones by writing me poison pen letters:

> Dear Sir:
> I going to be plain and to the point. I think that you are a stupid nut. I live in South Carolina but am station in Florida in the Air Force.
> I guess every time a cow, hog, horse, or a dog has to take a piss or shit youre going to run out and unzip their pants or pull them down. Please reply with your answer. I think your crazy as Hell!!
> > Sincerelly,
> > H. K.

Dear Lame Brain:

If I was the President I would shoot your ass off. Who ever was so dum as to start that crap of animals wearing pants! Boy, even back in Jesus Christ time here on earth, he never said clothe the animals. So if he didn't think it was indecent, why does a bunch of Nuts like you try something like this? Get gone you dam nuts.

What the Hell are you Comminist or some crazy cult?

(Unsigned)

Wiggins, Mississippi

Dear Mr. Abble:

If you really want to do something for humanity why don't you start a drive to get some pants and bra's on most of the women running around today? Go into most any restaurant or bus or any public place and just take a look when the women sit down. With their short skirts you can easily see that they have no pants on and with their plunging neck lines you just know they have no bra's on.

Believe me, the half naked women of today bother men more today than naked animals do. I know.

S.H.

Santa Monica, California

Dear Mr. Abel:

I would like to invite you to be our guest speaker at the Christ Church Communion breakfast this Sunday at 9:30 A.M. The meeting will end at 10:50 to allow time to go into the 11:00 A.M. church service. It will be a pleasure to have you and I certainly hope you can make it.

Sincerely yours,

H. H.

President, Men's Council

I didn't think it was proper for me to talk about clothing naked animals so early in the morning, especially on a Sunday and in a Presbyterian church. So I graciously declined the invitation. But I did accept one from the All

Souls Unitarian Church on Lexington Avenue in New York. This was a Sunday afternoon and I baffled their congregation for more than an hour before confessing they had been had. During the put-on portion one woman made a dramatic protest by walking out directly in front of the speakers' rostrum. A man in the last row read a book throughout.

Just to test the moral fiber of nudists—and their sense of humor—I wrote a dozen of the largest camps in New Jersey and Arizona to warn them I would take away their volleyballs if they didn't cover all vital areas forthwith, including those of their pets. This was one of several answers:

Dear Mr. Abel:

Don't know how you got our address in New York unless you are going to bed at night looking at nudist magazines. You say that you have turned down offers to visit nudist resorts. Too bad that you hate to meet people with clean minds.

The only way you can visit us, is your wife would have to be with you. You would like nudists resorts closed. The one place were clean minded, honest people can go, and not have any fear of drunks, thiefs or anybody making a pass at your wife.

If you are serious in this work, you really must have a twisted brain, and hope your cell is well padded, when they put you away. In case you are doing this for publicity and fun or with the idea of people sending you money, good. If they are that simple minded, they don't need the money anyway.

Come to Phoenix and we will put some clothes on the horses and other pets, probably get a dairy to dress their cows for you. There will be a small condition. You will be the one that has to do the laundry.

Out of curisoty, how long is the lace on your shorts? Maybe, you can't stand the sight of a bare leg and wear long underwear. Bet it would be fun to watch you take a bath with your clothes on.

Don't try changing the U.S.A., just for you, go buy a island and live to suit yourself. Have met a few people in my life that didn't seem to be all there, but guess you take the cake.

Goodbye Mama's little prud and have fun. Come X-mas, will try to send you a ball with some jacks to play with.

> Yours truly,
> H.M.
> Nudist Ranch

There were also people who not only believed I was sincere in wanting to clothe all animals for the sake of decency, but shared my concern and offered substantial financial aid. One woman in Santa Barbara, California, contacted me through her attorney with a check for forty thousand dollars! Was somebody putting me on for a change? Could this be a test, a trap or what?

I was in San Francisco at the time, en route to Los Angeles, so I arranged to meet with the donor and her attorney in Santa Barbara. She turned out to be a wealthy dowager who was particularly concerned about the neighbors' naked animals that came into her yard. Her lawyer was a straightlaced fellow with the necessary papers (affording his client a nice tax deduction for her charitable donation) properly drawn up and ready for my signature with no strings attached. This was no joke!

In order not to embarrass the woman by explaining she had been twaddled by a put-on, I told her that the constitution and bylaws of our organization forbade me to accept any money from strangers. She and her lawyer both looked at me incredulously.

"Obviously," I went on, "I can only accept your money

if you are a relative. So, since you are not related to me, I can't accept your money. But I appreciate the thought. Perhaps you can give it to some other worthwhile cause like cancer research or leprosy."

She was terribly upset by my attitude—shouted that nobody had ever turned her down—stalked out of the lawyer's office mumbling to herself. As I watched her enter a chauffered limousine, the lawyer looked at me with disdain; probably more because of my refusal to accept his client's money than out of contempt for my ludicrous campaign. His look seemed to say, "If he won't take her money, then he must really be crazy, or up to no good." People do reason this way.

Even friends wonder aloud why I don't take the money I'm offered. And I must say I'm somewhat disappointed in them for asking. First of all, if I took such money, I'd have to *believe* in the cause, and that would be crazy. To accept money in the name of a nonexistent (however humorous) organization would be fraudulent. And I am not a fraud.

However, I've been accused of being a Communist, a pervert and everything elso that good clean Americans hold ugly. My sanity has been questioned, my manhood challenged and my life threatened.

Students at the University of British Columbia took my satirical lecture on the need to clothe naked animals so seriously that they almost threw me into their swimming pool in the dead of winter.

A threat on my life was made one night a few years ago when Les Crane called on me to substitute for Jack E. Leonard, who couldn't appear on his late night television show. Now Jack E. is a big man. He would be hard to replace, but I thought I'd try. However, I'm afraid I gave a much too convincing performance, for the celebrity guests of the show, Vaughn Meader and Mercedes Mc-Cambridge, both stormed out of the studio afterwards. And Vaughn remarked to Les, "I would have preferred Jack E. Leonard to this guy!"

It was not an uneven match, in that Mercedes was slinging some barbs of her own at me: "Have you ever seen a psychiatrist? And if so, is he still practicing?"

I protested, "Please, Miss McCambridge. I don't want to argue with you. After all, you've memorized wicked lines from old Joan Crawford movies you can use against me!"

It went on like that all evening as callers on this phone-in show indicated that friends had awakened them to switch on their sets and watch the verbal fireworks. After the show Les was all smiles. As I started to leave the studio, his producer, Rudy Tellez, stopped me at the stage door and said I was going to have a police escort home. Apparently, somebody had called while the program was on the air and threatened I would be shot afterwards.

My first impulse was to fluff it off, reasoning that if anyone is to be feared, it's the deranged guy who doesn't call. And this character had probably already achieved his personal gratification during the phone call. Nevertheless, the cops were waiting and I decided to take a free ride home with New York's Finest. I didn't even have to tip.

Being a hoaxer has its risks. I've been blackballed from radio and television stations. Even magazines. When David A. Lyle, senior editor of the now defunct *Saturday Evening Post*, wrote a *Life* magazine editor that he might wish to cover one of my hoaxes, the reply was accidentally sent to me:

Dave:

It seems that *Life*'s own Jane Howard got somewhat taken in by one of Alan's little put-ons (maybe it was even a big put-on, I don't know the details). At any rate Dave Scherman (CLOSE UPS) won't touch Alan, not even with a cattle prod!

I well remembered the incident with Jane Howard. She and a photographer spent hours photographing our two dogs wearing Bermuda shorts, seemingly convinced that my wife and I were zany moral crusaders. She wrote her story, a four-page spread, and it was only hours away from going to press when somebody spotted the hoax and warned the editors just in time. It was a close call for *Life;* ditto *Time* and *Newsweek* magazines, which were running similar stories and managed to save face at the zero hour by printing the truth, or their version of it.

During the summer of 1965, on an all-night talk show over a radio station in New York City, I advocated draining the water from Long Island Sound into huge barrage balloons to be suspended overhead. I proposed to erect high-rise apartment buildings on the dry bed of the sound to spread out the congested city population.

My cohorts for this little travesty were independent film producer Robert Downey; humorist George Wayne; and my wife, Jeanne, who played the role of an eighty-six-year-old senior citizen, Cynthia Lansing York.

Prior to going on the air, we developed the following routine rehearsing in our apartment.

"I still don't understand what you're going to do with all that water in the sound," protested Downey.

"People can take all they want for their lawns," I explained.

"But that's salt water," he argued. "You're going to kill the grass!"

"Why not freeze the water?" interjected George Wayne. "Everyone knows that icebergs contain less salt than the water which it was. Then the icebergs could just be hauled by tugboat out to sea . . . or maybe the ice could be sold to the Fulton Fish Market."

"What about the people who want to swim?" asked Downey.

"Haven't you ever heard of swimming pools?" I said facetiously. "I think the water could be gotten rid of by means of artificial evaporation. . . ."

"But that method would probably cause excessive rain-fall on the surrounding states," interrupted Wayne with mock seriousness. "Maybe even cause a great flood. I suggest that we raise the land under the water, so when it rises up, the water would safely drain off."

"You can't raise the ground up!" shouted Downey angrily. "Who ever heard of such a thing?"

"Moles can do it," retorted Wayne sharply. "Is man any less inferior?"

"And you're supposed to be an engineer!" said Downey sarcastically.

"I stand on my record, Mr. Downey," answered Wayne coolly, "which is more than you can say! I happened to see your last film . . . and I'm sure it was."

We were finding it difficult not to laugh at this travesty, particularly when Jeanne spoke in a quivering voice as the senior citizen:

"I'd like to read a poem. A snake crawled up on my porch and died last night. And it set me to a-wondering. Who did he love, this little snake? On moonlit nights. Who did he cuddle round, and round, and round?"

Nobody spoke for a second or two. George Wayne cleared his throat and I continued the conversation:

"I think the problem of the disposal of water from Long Island Sound could easily be accomplished by loading it aboard Pennsylvania Railroad tank cars. It might even help the railroad get back on its feet. Or it could simply be piped to a drought area . . . like New York."

"New York is a drought area?" asked Downey incredulously.

"Have you ever thought about how many toilet flushes there are every day in New York City?" I suggested.

"No," he said. "Such trivia doesn't interest me."

"Multiply eight million people by at least six times a day," I exclaimed, "and that's a lot of trivia!"

"Maybe," replied Downey slyly. "But there are a lot of people who don't flush."

This farcical concept was broadcast for five hours through the night and was embellished with other suggestions from time to time. For instance, the necessary landfill for the drained sound was to be bought from the state of West Virginia because it could use the money. And for the people who would miss the sight of water, I planned to hire fifty artists to paint a backdrop of the sound which would be wrapped around the buildings.

The next day the New York District Attorney's office was bombarded with complaints from worried citizens along the North Shore of Long Island. They insisted some madman intended to drain their beautiful sound. An assistant D.A. demanded a recording of the program and started an investigation—which was dropped like a lead barrage balloon when he listened to the entire tape.

This particular show over WOR Radio was hosted by

"The Amazing Randi" and pulled more mail than any other single program in the station's history. It was presented deadpan, without being introduced as a spoof, so a lot of people didn't perceive the satire. I suspect more would have had they tuned in this wacky discussion on a familiar comedy TV show. But outside that recognizable framework—and without a laugh track—most listeners took our nonsense seriously.

Other zany ideas we introduced on the same show included an electronic bird watcher (for lazy people who liked birds but didn't want to waste time watching) and a plan by which people could live under water by having gills transplanted in their necks.

"But wouldn't small fish have a tendency to swim into your mouth?" asked panelist George Wayne.

"Well, that's the fish's problem, not mine," I countered.

"Living under water would eliminate laundry problems," offered producer Downey, "not to mention the savings on talcum powder."

Randi concluded the show with comments in defense of the put-on. He argued that "satire is valuable because it tears down and reduces to rust all these many brass idols that we construct out of our own clay and worship, whether they be political idols or moral statues."

He repeated a tape of this program several weeks later and included some of the hostile telegrams that came in ("I've been listening to this trash for the past two hours and I am now switching to another station") along with complimentary letters:

> I can't remember when I enjoyed a radio program more. I sat in my bedroom with the tears pouring down my cheeks, convulsing with laughter. Certainly I and those like me enjoyed the show innumerable times more

than those poor benighted souls who haven't the capacity to recognize and appreciate satire. But then I suppose if it wasn't for them, there would be no purpose for satire. I'm sure there are people who heard the show, heard the give-away ending, and *still* didn't get the joke!

Sincerely,
N.C.
New York City

How listeners can take Alan Abel and his cohorts seriously is hard to understand. Except that Americans have taken seriously Father Coughlin, Goat-gland Brinkley, Amy Semple McPherson and Pie-in-the Sky Townsend. Even if you have given it away, Randi, please bring Mr. Abel and his friends back; it is something to laugh about when there is such little cause in our world today for mirth. Thank you for all the pleasure you have given me.

Sincerely,
D.M.
New York City

In Cleveland, Ohio, a man tried to give me a thousand dollars for the fictitious Mrs. Yetta Bronstein's Presidential campaign. His offer came right on the air during a mock political speech I was making—as Yetta's campaign manager—on the *Alan Douglas Show*. Later I answered the phone in the producer's office and the same man repeated his pledge. After a few minutes of conversation there was no question but that this man was serious.

So I told him, "I appreciate your offer sir. But I must advise you that Mrs. Bronstein will only accept donations that are made up of unmarked used bills, in five- and ten-dollar denominations, that are bundled and thrown from a moving car traveling at least sixty miles an hour. Your drop zone would be near a Sohio gasoline station in

Cleveland Heights between 5 and 6 A.M. tomorrow. Are you still interested?"

The poor man panicked, refused to donate anything under those strange conditions and quickly withdrew his offer.

"Then how do you earn a living?" strangers often ask me after a television broadcast or a luncheon where I have just spoken. They fail to consider that the speaker's fee just given me is a perfectly good source of income. When I point this out, people still ask, "Yes. But I mean, what do you *really* do for a living?" Funny thing is, after hearing one of my put-on lectures, nobody seems to believe anything I say.

Over the past ten years I have spoken before several thousand schools, colleges, clubs and community organizations throughout the country, and on at least three hundred radio and television programs. Although I occasionally lecture straight on serious subjects, many a program chairman hires me because he wants to vicariously pull the legs of his friends and colleagues. As has happened so often, the audiences are unaware of the put-on—figuring some nutty professor type had been booked by mistake—until I eventually confess the hoax.

When I spoke at the Harvard Club in New York for the American Association of Pediatric Surgeons as a moral crusader, the three hundred doctors and their wives present were convinced I was a nut—as many confessed to me afterwards—yet they laughed and applauded throughout, even when I touched a sensitive nerve:

"Recently I advised key members of the American Medical Association that all doctors should be required by law to publish their college grades in the telephone directory after their names. This way, anyone could quickly determine the skill and price of a doctor. A surgeon with A-plus following his name would certainly be more trustworthy in performing a delicate brain operation—and be allowed to charge more—than the doctor who scraped through college on D-minus. Think of the ease with which people could then choose their medical specialists from the yellow pages. . . ."

During the question and answer period there were some lively exchanges:

"Mr. Abel," one of the doctors' wives asked facetiously, "don't you think your ideas are just a little too progressive for intelligent human beings to accept?"

"Just put me in a room alone with you for two hours and I'm sure I could convert you to my way of thinking," I replied with a straight face. The audience exploded with laughter.

A doctor sitting near the speakers' dais didn't mince words: "Have you ever thought of getting help?"

"Sir, I'll have you know that I have been often examined by a duly qualified psychiatrist who happens to live right down the hall from me in my apartment building. We have a wonderful deal, I trade him trumpet lessons for an hour on his couch every Wednesday. He has pronounced me perfectly sane."

"He must be a hell of a lousy trumpet player," quipped the doctor in a loud voice that brought the house down with laughter and applause.

When the program chairmen, Dr. Anthony Shaw and Dr. Thomas Santulli, revealed my true identity, the audience responded with pleasure at learning their collective legs had been pulled. And relief to know I was a joker and not an escapee from a mental institution.

Sometimes my activities have been confused with those

of Fred "Ferdinand" Demara, known as "The Great Impostor." Demara has achieved notoriety for his masquerades as a surgeon, a priest and a teacher because he not only intentionally assumed the credentials of living professionals but also practiced their trades using their very own names! And with great skill, according to those who knew his talents.

A recent newspaper account quoted Demara as saying: "People have the idea I went through life thumbing my nose at officialdom. That's not so. My life really has been a series of tragedies. I have been misquoted and lied about and I would like not to have any story at all. And although I have been described as a working impostor, I have found needs and tried to fulfill them."

Tragic but true. Demara has great natural abilities and performed better than many men with the proper academic training and degrees required by law. The framed medical diploma on the wall of a doctor's office may permit him to make all kinds of boners and go without punishment, but the lack of that sheepskin earned Demara the wrath of the law.

Unlike Demara's earnest efforts to perform as a doctor, my role as a psychologist was assumed for entertainment only—on television—with a revelation at the end to make sure no one took my absurd philosophy literally. One such assignment was on *The Dick Cavett Show* when producer Woody Fraser secretly hired me to play a social psychologist and fool Cavett on April Fool's Day. After being introduced by the host, I sat down next to his other guests, Arlene Francis and Trini Robb, sister-in-law of Lynda Johnson Robb.

"Tell us about your research, Dr. Spencer," Cavett said.

"I understand you have some interesting views on the subject of pornography."

"I'll be happy to," I replied soberly. "I've just spent the past six months researching a subject in this country that is generally considered taboo. And I have here today the findings that I think many are going to find shocking. I found out in my study that 92 per cent of the people in this country want hardcore pornography. So why should a minority of moral maniacs deny what the masses want? They shouldn't. I have here a pornochart. This horizontal line shows that people didn't know they wanted pornography because nobody ever asked them. When I asked them, the line immediately shot up off the board. Which proves my point that you can't hide behind a broomstick anymore. Furthermore, by making pornography legal we'll keep perverts off the streets at night. They'll read at night and spend their days shopping for dirty books."

Cavett looked at me incredulously, Arlene Francis crossed her legs cautiously and Trini Robb coughed nervously. I went right on, speaking with authority:

"I think we should legalize pornography. Here is another chart showing four hundred peeping toms. Now where do you go to find a prime group of peeping toms? Well, we put innocent ads in the paper that said there was going to be a hot party in a certain penthouse. And for all Peeping Toms to bring along their binoculars and meet on a nearby rooftop. In later tests we found that after the peeping toms were given dirty books to read, their interest in peeping went down to zero."

"Are you for real?" asked Cavett with suspicion.

"Yes," I replied, feigning a wounded pride.

"I'm sorry," he apologized.

"I would like to point out that the people in this very audience came here to see a dirty show," I continued. "When they look at you, Dick Cavett, they don't see you. No. They see Richard Nixon frolicking in the nude! It's true. And when they look at Arlene Francis here—if I may give my opinion—they see Elizabeth Taylor in the shower. You see, we have to come out and be honest. Did I hear someone in the audience say I had a dirty mind? Well let me tell you, lady, if you think that thinking dirty is dirty, then you're thinking dirty. That means exactly what it means. Now I have compiled all my statistics in this little black book that contains all the results of my survey. We're not going to hide behind anything. This is a dirty, rotten, filthy book. And I would like to ask you several questions, Mr. Cavett, although I don't think they will be good for your image. You don't have to answer these. But this is the type question I asked my two thousand study groups. First, are you broadminded? How long is your indicating finger? Now of course I analyze the answers later. They wouldn't mean anything to me now. Have you ever dreamed of being chased by a snake? Have you ever been chaste? What part of a nude statue do you look at first? Second? Do you believe that abstinence makes the heart grow fonder? Who invented the pill? Jacqueline Susann? George Jessel? Or Charles de Gaulle? Well, that last one is a little tricky. We threw in some humor just to ease the tension. Was Lady Godiva an equestrian? An exhibitionist? Or overheated? And here's the final one. True or false. Castration is a form of government in Cuba. Now, this is my *Dirty, Rotten, Filthy Book,* which I'm not ashamed to show here publicly for the first time. It was just published today and contains the kind of pornographic information any Decent Literature Group would want to examine. It is already banned in Boston. Because it also contains such sordid facts as the 32,000 obscene phone calls made in New York City last year. We learned that 23 per cent of them were *collect* calls!

"Are you a gag?" shouted Cavett above the laughter of the audience.

"Yes," I confessed, "and it's your April Fool's Day present."

"Well, I've got a surprise for you," said Cavett with feigned anger. "You're not going to get paid! Who the hell are you anyway?"

I explained that my performance was arranged by his producer, Woody Fraser, and Cavett remarked that I did bear a resemblance to Arlene Francis' husband.

"Well, not as far as dirty books are concerned, if you don't mind!" snapped Miss Francis, apparently annoyed by my stand on pornography.

Cavett avoided any exchanges between us as he went quickly to a commercial. Then he told the audience, "The gentleman who put me on so rottenly was Alan Abel. I was absolutely convinced. I thought he was cuckoo and all sorts of things. And this *Dirty, Rotten, Filthy Book* is the title of his book. And it's something the whole family can enjoy, apparently. You really are Alan Abel, aren't you, unless this is *another* April Fool and you're Allan Funt."

"No, I'm really me," I said convincingly.

TWO

I KIDNAPED
GENE KRUPA

I pulled off the first stunt of what has become a career
not for the sake of hoaxing but to avoid being labeled
a hoaxer. While a student at Ohio State University I
founded the Jazz Forum on campus in 1947 to give weekly
jazz concerts every Saturday afternoon on the stage of
University Hall, an auditorium that seated about twelve
hundred.

At first I featured local jam sessions, which were quite
disorganized. Anybody with an instrument was welcome
to play and sometimes only trumpets showed up. But
by the end of the first year—a time when postwar jazz had
started to flourish—I found myself with a production staff
of forty students. Thereafter, our concerts were well
planned and always played to a full house.

Whenever name bandleaders appeared in or around Columbus, Ohio, I would persuade them to visit the campus and lecture before a Jazz Forum audience. The lecture, as I well anticipated, always turned into a jam session with student musicians. One summer alone we had Elliot Lawrence, Ray Anthony, Charlie Spivak, Jimmy Dorsey and Norman Granz's *Jazz at the Philharmonic* troupe.

When I learned that Gene Krupa was scheduled at Buckeye Lake Park I was particularly interested in inviting him to appear at Ohio State, for I, too, played the drums. I phoned his manager and he agreed to send Krupa over to speak on a Saturday afternoon two weeks away, allowing that it wouldn't interfere with his nightly band performance and would be good public relations. (Krupa still had the stigma of a marijuana charge over his head, for which he served ninety days in a San Francisco jail.)

Our Jazz Forum staff decided to go all out for this particular concert. We proclaimed Saturday "Gene Krupa Day" on our posters (we always proclaimed a day for any celebrity speaker to make sure he would show up) passed out handbills, sent news releases to newspapers and radio stations, even painted a special backdrop in his honor. Artist Glenn Wasserman, a pupil of Roy Lichtenstein, who was then teaching on campus, spent several afternoons with his canvas drop stretched out on the grass next to Derby Hall.

Admission to our concerts was by membership card only. It cost fifty cents to become a member, at the door, and the card expired right after the concert. This was one of the clever ways our student attorney arranged to avoid paying taxes. To assuage our consciences, we occasionally presented a benefit program with all proceeds going to a worthy cause such as the Damon Runyon Cancer Fund.

Many of our Jazz Forum associates went on to achieve national fame after college. Lee Adams wrote the lyrics for *Bye Bye Birdie* and *Golden Boy* on Broadway; Dean Miller became the romantic lead in television's *December Bride;* Dwike Mitchell was the first American jazz pianist to concertize in Russia; Harry Arouh joined CBS-TV as a featured reporter; and Calvin Mayne, another pianist, became an editor with the Rochester *Times*.

The day before Krupa's appearance we were assured of a capacity crowd; the campus buzzed with excitement over the pending arrival of the "King of the Drums." Around dinner time I called Krupa's manager at the Buckeye Lake Park ballroom and he was very angry with me.

"What the hell you kids doing up there?" he demanded to know. "I read in the Columbus *Dispatch* all about the concert and somebody sent me a poster. I never told you for sure Gene was coming up, so forget it! Besides, he has a very important meeting tomorrow afternoon with Billy Goodheart at his farm and it's a long drive from here."

I was stunned. Speechless. "But you promised," I pleaded.

"I promised I'd try, I didn't say I would," the manager said. And then he hung up.

I was furious. Not only because he wasn't keeping his word but because when several of Krupa's band were ill, I'd sent him Jazz Forum musicians as substitutes. How could I ever explain the latest turn of events to my staff? And what about the students who were bound to turn out en masse for the concert?

Billy Goodheart was a name I knew in music circles as a

former executive with Music Corporation of America who was in semiretirement on a farm in Eaton, Ohio. I decided to call him. Perhaps I could convince him to persuade Krupa not to cancel out on our concert. Then the thought came to me that the manager might be bluffing; maybe Krupa wasn't going anywhere. So I placed a person-to-person call for Gene Krupa at Goodheart's farm.

"Gene Krupa?" I heard a voice ask the operator. "He isn't here. He's up at Buckeye Lake with his band. Who's calling?"

I gave my name to the operator and asked if I could reach him at this number tomorrow.

"No," said Goodheart. "I don't expect him here tomorrow either. We just had a meeting last weekend."

He had lied to me. But why? Well, that didn't matter now. There was only one solution: I had to kidnap Gene Krupa. But I couldn't do it alone. I needed lots of help. Although it took the rest of the night to make all the phone calls, by 10 A.M. the next morning, the entire Jazz Forum staff had assembled in front of the house where I had a basement apartment. Parked on the street were a dozen cars, mostly convertibles, including a 1929 Essex open touring car owned and driven by "Fearless" Jimmy Ruffner. Six beautiful coeds, led by campus queen Ronnie Denune, were on hand; Ziggy Coyle and Paul DeFrancis had their musical combos; Glenn Wasserman's signs were everywhere, wrapped around the cars, on broomsticks and being worn as sandwich signs: "Welcome to OSU, Gene Krupa"—"We Love You, Gene"—"Gene Krupa Day at OSU."

I explained to the entourage that we were going to give Gene Krupa the kind of welcome he deserved, that it wasn't enough for us just to let him drive alone to the campus, that we were going out to greet him and escort him back like royalty. The crowd cheered its approval, not suspecting what I had in store for them or Krupa. Our college enthusiasm was par for the course in those days.

Privately, I explained to the girls that we wanted to surprise Mr. Krupa and they should use their feminine charms to make him feel wanted. I mentioned he was bashful, would probably resist their attentions and they were to use all necessary means to transport him safely into one of the cars.

During the drive out to Buckeye Lake Park we picked up two motorcycle policemen for an escort along Route 40 (they were friends of one of our staff members). With flags and banners waving, pretty coeds cheering and the two bands playing almost continuously, we were quite a spectacle along the highway. Traffic slowed and people strained their necks to see who all the fuss was over.

We arrived at Krupa's lakeside hotel in an hour. It was noontime, only two hours until the concert. As pre-planned, the cars drew up in a large circle right underneath Krupa's third-floor room, which faced the rear parking lot. The combined bands swung into "When the Saints Go Marching In," everybody clapped hands, the girls smiled and we all waited for the maestro to appear.

Employees from the hotel and guests came running outside to see what the excitement was all about. Krupa's nose and eyes appeared between two parted Venetian blinds. Good. He was still in his room and now there was no time to lose. I quickly signaled the band to leave their open cars and wind inside the hotel, around through the lobby, performing a snake dance. Away they went with the girls right behind. The drivers stayed in their cars, all engines running, pointed toward the exit ramp leading back to Columbus.

Pandemonium reigned inside the lobby. This was the height of the summer tourist season and the weekend was particularly busy. With the band blaring fortissimo, a horde of people milled around in front of the main desk, and business for the Lake Breeze Hotel came to a complete standstill. The manager asked, "Who's in charge here?" and I was pointed out. He came toward me, shouted something in my ear, but I couldn't hear a word. From the scowl on his face, however, I could see he wasn't very happy.

To keep the manager occupied temporarily while the girls went upstairs to Krupa's room, I shook his hand vigorously and shouted loudly, "What a great day this is for you and your hotel, sir. Imagine the thrill of having Gene Krupa staying with you and now to be so honored in this fashion. As the official host I want to wish you the best of luck and congratulate you on the fine job you are doing for this establishment. . . ."

I didn't let go of his hand, just kept talking, while keeping an eye on the staircase. I'm still uncertain how the girls managed it. But Krupa finally appeared in the lobby dressed in a white suit. He seemed groggy-eyed and in a state of semishock as twelve feminine hands soothed his brow and half-carried him out to the waiting Essex convertible. There his protests were smothered with hugs and kisses and compliments. So far, these lovely queens had performed with all the perfection of a Woody Hayes football team!

Our musicians and followers finished their snake dance and hurried back to the cars. The last to leave the hotel, I ran squarely into Krupa's manager. He looked at me dumbfounded, impotent in his wet swim trunks. Somebody had summoned him from the swimming pool, but he was too late. Nevertheless, he created a small scene of his own standing in the center of the lobby, dripping wet, barefooted, with a glass diving mask on the top of his head. As he shouted angry words at me and shook with rage, I stood my ground.

"Listen, you lied to me and your bluff didn't work. I called Billy Goodheart and he said Krupa wasn't expected." Then I turned away and headed for my caravan.

I jumped into the back seat of the Essex with two of the girls. Krupa was jammed in the front with two more and driver Ruffner. Away we went. The two motorcycle policemen had been waiting on the highway, which was about a mile from the hotel, so they had no inkling of what had just taken place. It was close to 1 P.M. and we were an hour's drive from the campus for our 2 P.M. concert.

The musicians continued to play as we drove. Nobody in our car said anything for the first twenty minutes. Then Krupa turned around to me.

"This is kidnaping, you know."

"I'm sorry about all this, Mr. Krupa," I said. I hoped that once we reached University Hall and he saw the large crowds he would have a change of heart and cooperate with us.

"Can you push this thing a little faster?" I urged Jimmy Ruffner and he nodded and pressed down on the accelerator. We zoomed from a fast forty miles per hour to fifty-

five and there was a loud *pop!* Rust-colored water from
the overheated radiator squirted all over Krupa, narrowly
missing the girls. Ruffner slammed on the brakes and
pulled off the road, followed by the whole caravan.

Everybody piled out and gathered around our car. The
motorcycle policemen came running with a first-aid kit.
Krupa stood on the running board, his suit ruined. One
of the musicians produced a Turkish towel and a track
suit from the trunk of his car. Krupa went into the bushes
and changed clothes while the girls stood nearby, in case
he also decided to do a little running.

There was a pay phone booth a few hundred feet ahead
and I sprinted for it. We were going to be twenty or thirty
minutes late and I wanted to alert Glenn Wasserman back
at University Hall, who was in charge on that front. He
answered on the first ring.

"Glenn, we got him! Go to work. See you in about
thirty."

Back to the cars. I suggested Krupa transfer to a newer
model. No, he liked the old one and climbed into the
back seat, where I joined him. The sweat suit fitted quite
well and I assured Krupa we would pay for any damages
to his clothes.

"You know," he said, looking straight ahead, "I don't
intend to perform or speak or anything when we get to
your college. I'm going under protest. So you might as
well get that straight right now."

"Look, Gene," I said, "we only have a short time, so
please hear me out. Then you can do whatever you feel
is fair."

I explained what had transpired with his manager and
my phone call to Billy Goodheart. Krupa listened but

didn't comment until I concluded with, "And so I figured the only way to save the situation was to come out and get you in this fashion."

"I didn't know a thing about your concert," he said quietly. "But I still don't intend to perform, because this just isn't the way I do business."

We reached the stage door of University Hall twenty-five minutes late. Inside, Pfc. Dwike Mitchell and the Lockbourne Air Base band were playing one of his original jazz tunes before a jam-packed audience. It was our largest crowd in two years. I led Krupa to a private dressing room backstage and two girls remained outside as an honor guard. He motioned for me to come inside.

"I told you I wasn't going out there on stage and I mean it."

Somebody handed a suit in through the door that was Krupa's size, but he waved it away, turned around to look out the window and lit a cigarette. I decided to try a final pitch because it was now or never.

"That day at the Paramount Theater in New York when you rode up on the band elevator with the great Tommy Dorsey Orchestra and electrified the audience, not only with your presence but your ability on the drums . . . well, Gene . . . you have a similar situation here today. Everybody out there knows about your trouble on the West Coast but they don't know the truth. From what I've heard you were urged by your own attorney to plead guilty to the possession of marijuana charge in order to avoid a sensational newspaper trial and receive instead a suspended sentence. But there was a political doublecross involved and you had to serve ninety days.

"So if you leave now—since they all know you're here— you'll give that audience the erroneous impression you're ashamed to face them. And they will associate that action with your guilty plea. They want to see you, hear you, that's why they came. How can you let them down now? And I've always believed that in the highest tradition of show business, the show must go on. That's all I have to say."

Krupa turned around slowly and eyed me coldly. "Right now I'm thinking of summoning my lawyer to start legal action against you, your Jazz Forum and the college. Not to mention a federal charge of kidnaping. While I'm figuring out what to do, why don't you go out there on stage and give me an introduction?"

My mind froze for a second in disbelief, then I came back to life, gave Krupa a whack on the back that nearly sent him sprawling, and I dashed out on stage right in the middle of the band's sixth number. They stopped abruptly and I gave my shortest introduction ever:

"And now, here he is, Gene Krupa!"

As Krupa headed toward the stage, still dressed in the sweatsuit, the entire audience rose to its feet and welcomed him with sustained applause. He hesitated at hearing the thunderous reception, looked back at me, smiled, shook his head incredulously, and strode out in front of the cheering fans, who ended their spontaneous ovation with "three cheers for Gene Krupa!"

Just before Krupa began to speak, a large shaggy dog came in through one of the opened fire exit doors, sat down on the stage and stared up at him. It couldn't have been better if planned. The dog's attitude of rapt attention broke the ice. Krupa laughed openly with the audience as our stage manager, Don Dupre, led the dog outside.

For nearly forty minutes Krupa explained his philosophy of music and answered questions from the audience. One student asked if he would play a drum solo or two. Krupa's reply was firm: "I came here to lecture, not to play." The audience quickly registered its disappointment. Somebody began to chant, "We want a drum solo, we want a drum solo," which was soon picked up by others until the auditorium rocked with the request.

Backstage behind the closed curtains I had already made plans for Krupa to play. My own drums were set up in the same manner as his. And most of Krupa's musicians were lined up as well, instruments ready, to begin playing "C Jam Blues." (Concerned about the fate of their leader, they had followed our caravan at a safe distance all the way from Buckeye Lake.) When the curtains opened, Krupa was again trapped, this time in the middle of a swinging jam session. He shrugged, sat down at the drums and played magnificently—including an exciting ten-minute solo.

For a final few choruses, our *Jazz Forum* musicians joined in with Krupa's band, and University Hall's rafters really shook. Hopefully, this particular music session was not responsible for the later condemnation of the building as being "unsafe for occupancy!"

I stood in the wings on stage right while some fifteen musicians blew their heads off; in my direct line of vision on stage left I could see the form of a familiar figure snapping his fingers and tapping his toes in time to the music—Krupa's manager! And all smiles, too! Just like the happy ending in one of those old Judy Garland–Mickey Rooney movies.

Afterwards I met Krupa backstage in his dressing room surrounded by well-wishers, autograph hounds and musicians. The track suit he had worn on stage turned out to be just right for the occasion because he was soaked with perspiration. As he wiped his face with a towel, Krupa shouted at me above the voices and general confusion: "How would you like to manage a dance band?"

I was tempted momentarily, but I'd already resolved to get a college degree. We shook hands good-by just as his manager came in to offer congratulations to everyone for an exciting concert. He even had a few kind words for me.

Today, whenever I meet Gene Krupa in New York, the first thing he does is look around in all directions—hoping, no doubt, there might be six beautiful girls ready to abduct him.

THREE

MY AGENT—
BRUCE SPENCER

I have one of the best agents in the business—Bruce Spencer. He takes care of my bookings, my finances and my general well-being. He really likes me. And I trust him. When someone wants my services, whether it be for writing or performing, he's a tough bargainer. Bruce does most of his negotiating and selling by telephone. And hardly any business acquaintance can remember having met him. The only one who knows him intimately is his chief client, Alan Abel. The reason for this secrecy? I am also "Bruce Spencer."

Friends who know about my double role often ask why I don't sign a management contract with an ordinary agent. The answer is simple. With Bruce fronting for me,

I have complete independence, the right to run my own life. To work when I want, for whom I want. Furthermore, it's because of my past experience with agents, both large and small, that I created my own agent.

When I first came to New York in the early fifties, I had developed a comedy act with the snare drum—in the style of Victor Borge's routine with the piano. I called an agent named Meyer North, who told me to rent a room so he could audition my act. I was so naïve I thought "a room" meant a hotel room. So I rented a room at the Hotel Taft and left word with North's answering service. I waited all day for him. He never showed up.

Yet another agent advised me to rent a room for a private audition to work at the swank Boca Raton Country Club in Florida. By this time I understood that "a room" was a rehearsal hall. I rented the finest available on Broadway by the hour, including a small stage, plenty of room to project and a miniature spot light. It was very professional of me. I waited all afternoon and that evening, but he didn't show up either. My bank account was fast dwindling and I hadn't even been heard yet!

The third time around agent Jules Ziegler actually appeared and seemed impressed. He booked me in Quebec at a French-Canadian night club where the patrons understood very little English. For an entire week I gave them a monologue in English on "the history of the snare drum and its effect on civilization today" while they ate and talked quietly in French. Although this scene made no sense to me, it did to the manager of the club. He insisted I uphold my contract because he wanted somebody on stage during the dinner show to watch and make sure nobody skipped out without paying the check!

Another agent booked me as an after-dinner speaker

before an orthodox Zionist gathering where only Yiddish was spoken. When I went into my monologue the audience kept right on talking in their native tongue. After ten minutes of this multilingual fugue, I said several *shalom aleichem's* and departed. Everybody applauded, probably out of relief because I no longer interrupted their conversations!

I decided to give the agents one more chance. This time it was a firm headed by a well-known Broadway producer and the millionaire art patron Walter Chrysler, who included among his collection a building bearing his name. They signed me up with glowing promises for a period of five years and demanded only 15 per cent of my income for their exclusive services. The management contract covered all phases of the entertainment field—radio, television, theater, films, recordings, commercials, concerts, night clubs—and I was promised an opportunity to appear in a forthcoming Broadway production.

A year went by. And the producer-patron team had come up with only one booking for me—a free benefit at the home of New York City's fire commissioner!

To pay the rent and eat during this lean period, I worked for the American Automobile Association. First they sent me to school for a week, where I memorized the names of cities and towns in America and learned how to draw a green line on a map with a Magic Marker. Then, every morning at 8:30 A.M. I sat around a table with twelve other college graduates and drew green lines on maps until noon. To make certain we didn't goof on the job, talking was prohibited. Our hands always had to be busy on top of the table and to ensure adherence to these rules, a supervisor (a high school graduate) strolled around the room slapping a ruler in the palm of his hand. It reminded me of the days when galley slaves rowed boats as the slavemaster walked up and down cracking his whip.

Six weeks of this tedium and I was ready to draw a green line on the supervisor. But I didn't have to do that. One morning among the letters dumped on my pile for processing, I found one written on engraved stationery. It was a request by a woman from Great Neck Estates for a map showing "the most scenic route from Great Neck, Long Island, to Newark, New Jersey." It was a distance of thirty miles as the crow flies (no reflection on the lady). She wanted a reply within four days because her chauffeur was going on vacation and the car would be put in storage for her six months' trip to Europe.

Well, a woman of such means should hardly be routed through the Holland or Lincoln Tunnels for a scenic trip to Newark! The short turnpike ride is mostly swamps, factories and nauseous odors. I didn't think the George Washington Bridge offered much "scenery" either.

So I sent her a map with a route that took her upstate New York, along the Hudson River, all the way to Montreal, and then back down on the western banks of the Hudson straight into Newark.

In my covering letter I added: "Consider the romance of Washington Irving's Hudson Valley, where the ghost of Ichabod Crane still roams; and Albany, where Robert Fulton's steamboat arrived from Jersey City in 1807. Today, this historical city is the center of industries producing toilet paper, dominoes and billiard balls. Burlington, Vermont, is the site of the oldest university and oldest daily newspaper in the state . . . and some of the oldest

people in the country. I suggest taking the ferry at Plattsburgh, New York, to get across the river . . . then on up
to Montreal.

"In Lake Placid, on your trip back down, is the home
of the noted abolitionist, John Brown; at Lake George,
the site of battles of the French and Indian War, you can
see demonstrations of cannon firing, musket firing and
bullet molding. Don't fail to visit Saratoga Springs for a
bath in the mineral waters. And I know you won't want
to miss stopping at West Point for the daily flag-raising
ceremony."

All in all, it was a pleasant two-day trip and a night's
layover in Canada with her chauffeur.

When I was summoned by my superior a few days later,
I entered his office walking on eggs. Literally. (I had
stepped on a co-worker's box lunch next to my chair.)
Something told me I was about to receive my walking
papers.

The woman was there—a living caricature of Great
Neck Estates. She was, as I had imagined, about seventy-
five, sitting sternly and rigid in her chair, holding a gold-
handled cane that was *tap, tap, tapping.* The purse of her
lips told me she was plainly upset. An Automobile Club
vice-president stood at her side and he wasted no time
with formalities, such as an introduction.

"Is this your initial on this map, Mr. Abel?"

"I believe it is, sir," I said, holding it up to the light.

"Do you have any explanation for your deplorable act?"

"Well, she did ask for the most scenic route to Newark
and I felt she should have a nice trip so I . . ."

"That will be all. Pick up your final check from the
cashier."

As I left to turn in my green Magic Marker, I heard

her say, "We were on the New York Thruway for an hour before I realized from the direction of the sun we were traveling in the wrong direction. Then James couldn't turn around on that awful turnpike, and that took another hour . . ."

What a relief to get back to show business full time! But my agents still hadn't found me any engagements. Only invitations to parties. Several other agents had expressed interest in my work but wouldn't handle me until I was free and clear of my current team. There were still four years to go on the contract and I was legally stuck.

As I reread the fine print in my contract, I realized my agents had the exclusive *right* to find me work but not the *obligation*. Yet I still had to pay them 15 per cent of my income from any kind of endeavor in the entertainment field, even if I paid another agent for finding me work. It didn't seem fair, but I had signed a contract and had to live with it unless I could obtain a release. Walter Chrysler wouldn't let me go. Nor would the producer. They both seemed to like me that much. I threatened to sue; they just laughed and pointed to my signature on the contract.

Taking a walk in Greenwich Village, I began to brood about the problem of how to dissolve my contract, even though my own lawyer said I had to sit it out and wait. But after you've spent four years in college and served three years in the service, to wait another four years before you can begin your life is a lot to ask. By the age of twenty-eight my life could be half over!

In Sheridan Square, sitting next to a sign that said *Do Not Feed The Pigeons,* was a raggedy man in his late sixties feeding the pigeons. An idea came to me. Such a man, I thought, would probably be willing to do just about anything for a few dollars.

"Pardon me, sir, but may I introduce myself?"

"I don't care what your name is," he said without looking up, still feeding bread crumbs to the birds. "I don't have a name anymore. I mean what's in a name? A name is a tag, that's all. It's what you feel and do that counts. If you really want to know who I am, I'm 032-18-0270."

"I couldn't agree with you more," I said. "But I'm looking for a man with a particular name, somebody who will be my press agent for only a few minutes. And I'm willing to pay five dollars for the service."

The man's eyes lit up and he stopped feeding the pigeons. "Five dollars, you said? What do I have to do?"

"Well," I answered, taking a piece of paper from my pocket and scribbling a few lines, "it's simple. I'm looking for a press agent who has the name Walter Chrysler. Now this is an agreement that says: 'I, Walter Chrysler of Sheridan Square Park, New York City, hereby agree to serve as Alan Abel's press agent for the sum of $5.' All you have to do is sign and the five dollars is yours."

He signed it and now I had proof that I had a press agent named Walter Chrysler. We shook hands good-by and I left him feeding the pigeons.

Next I visited a Times Square printer who worked a hand press in a two-by-four shop. There wasn't room inside for the customer so I had to stand on the street and hand him my order through a small window in the glass door. For three dollars, while I waited, he printed up one hundred sheets of paper with the heading in bold type: PUBLICITY BY WALTER CHRYSLER, SHERIDAN SQUARE PARK, NEW YORK CITY.

My first press release went out that night to columnists Walter Winchell, Earl Wilson and Ed Sullivan with the following copy:

FOR IMMEDIATE RELEASE

Humorist Alan Abel will perform completely nude in the Holland Tunnel at high noon next Thursday. His dramatic performance will include readings from Shakespeare, several operatic arias and a routine with a trained dog who can also catch fleas in midair and do backward somersaults. A collection will be taken from the motorists who are in the tunnel at the time and Mr. Abel will turn over 25 per cent of his money to the British War Orphans Relief Fund for Canadian soldiers who fought on the American side during the Korean War.

For further details contact Mr. Abel's press agent: WALTER CHRYSLER.

Two days later around seven-thirty in the morning I was awakened by a phone call from Walter Chrysler. The one from the talent agency. He was furious and cursed me out royally, demanding to know if I had gone stark raving mad. He said I was going to be sued for libel, slander and other charges that I was too sleepy to hear. After he quieted down a bit I explained:

"Walter, you know how much I appreciate what you and Lennie have done for me over the past year. And I want to help you continue your good work on my behalf. So, by coincidence, I've located a free-lance press agent who just happens to have the same name as yours. Now he has all these marvelous ideas for promoting my image. So every time you read something insane in the papers that was placed there by my press agent, Walter Chrysler, it's not you. Understand?"

Walter understood. Two hours later in his office I had

a signed release from my contract with their management firm. And we all lived happily ever after. They were both happy to see me go. And I was happy to leave.

I felt free, my future was in my own hands. I began to have some luck with my comedy act by playing such clubs as the Blue Angel, Cafe Society Downtown, Number One Fifth Avenue, Birdland and the Reuben Bleu, all of which are now closed, though I hope not because of my efforts.

And I kept on auditioning. For everything—television, Broadway shows, commercials, benefits and even the USO. Yet I would rather entertain an audience of thousands than audition for one producer. It's perhaps the most frightening experience any performer can have. You are expected to be at your best under the worst possible conditions. There is no audience to relate to; your performance is constantly interrupted by phone calls, messengers, secretaries and drill hammers from the construction next door. And the reward is an invitation to come back again—for more of the same!

After the fifth or sixth audition for the same show, and the choice has been narrowed down to just a few, you sit at home and wait for the good news. No news is bad news. Everytime the phone rings you have a slight cardiac arrest. How should I sound? Indifferent? Busy? Eager? Impatient? But it's usually only Aunt Martha calling up to berate you for not giving up all this nonsense and going into medicine or law.

Perhaps the most frustrating experience is auditioning for a show many times, getting closer and closer, while more and more of the competition is eliminated, then striking out at the zero hour.

Such was my own case when one chance to "make good"

seemed to be within reach. I was being considered for a new network television program called *One Minute Please*. It was a comedy panel show whose participants would each draw a wacky subject out of a hat and then improvise a monologue on it for one minute without hesitation or repetition of ideas.

During one of my auditions for the program I selected the topic "How to tell the head of a worm from its tail," and I said: "First you pick him up in the middle and dangle him awhile to see which end is more active. If nothing happens, it's possible you picked up a dead worm. Put him or her on the table along side a piece of lettuce. Whichever end goes for the food, that's the head. If neither end moves, don't lose heart. It may have already eaten. Take a feather and tickle him in the middle. If he wiggles one end, that's the head, looking for a way out; if he wiggles both ends, forget this method and start over again. Take a fishing hook and point it at him. Whichever way the worm runs, it's headfirst. Unless, of course, he's a backward worm, in which case . . ."

It was my kind of show and the producer, Dan Goodman, presently a vice-president with Screen Gems, kept bringing me back for more auditions until he was completely satisfied I was right for the panel.

Others signed for the program were Hermione Gingold, Marc Connolly, Cleveland Amory, Alice Ghostley and the late Ernie Kovacs. I was the only unknown. But I felt my obscurity was soon to be rectified.

One day I received the call. Dan Goodman was asking me to "come on down and sign a contract for the show because it goes on the air in three weeks." This was it! The big break! I dashed out the door for a taxi and was in his office forty minutes later.

Now comes the unbelievable part of this story that is so improbable it could happen only in real life. During my forty-minute cab ride the show changed producers and developed a new policy: the panel was to be comprised of name stars only. I was out. I was also crushed. The fickle finger of fate had signaled, but it turned out to be the middle finger, making that familiar sign of contempt.

As things turned out I was not replaced, just eliminated from the panel. My depression lasted as long as the show—thirteen weeks.

The experience with *One Minute Please* left me feeling vulnerable to the uncertain whims of the theatrical currents. I needed a defense, a scapegoat, a middle man between me and the market place. I needed an agent. But I didn't *want* an agent, not if I could solve the problem in some other way.

Playing the part of my own agent happened gradually. At numerous auditions I had stood in line for hours only to be turned away because I wasn't represented by an agent. After seeing all those names on the assistant's clipboard, and beside each a "William Morris" or "Ashley Famous" or "General Artists," I felt defeated. As if I had been blackballed from the club.

And yet I'd often wondered if all those hundreds of performers were handled by only a few agencies, how could any one actor expect to receive his agent's individual attention? Obviously he couldn't. So I devised a plan to represent myself. Fortunately, I had a good friend at Young and Rubicam, one of the largest advertising agencies, who allowed me to borrow his telephone during his long lunch periods. Then I would call up a producer who was casting a show, give him any name that occurred to me at the time—I was careful to mention I was *at*, not *with,* Young and Rubicam—and tell him, or his casting director, "I want to send over a great kid. Does a monologue with the snare drum. Just what you're looking for."

Then I'd grab my drum and run over. The same casting assistants who barred me before now checked my name off their clipboards and opened the door to the producer's office. This technique resulted in bookings on television with such shows as *The Armstrong Circle Theater, Today* and *The Ed Sullivan Show;* also cruises to Bermuda, many one-night stands in the mountain resorts, college dates and eventually recording contracts for albums with RCA Victor, ABC-Paramount and Liberty Records.

After my friend at Young and Rubicam left for another agency in Detroit, I was earning enough money to afford both a part-time secretary and my own telephone-answering service to handle incoming calls. That's when I hired an exclusive agent, Bruce Spencer, borrowed from my brother's first and middle names.

For the past ten years my agent and I have gotten along magnificently. He understands the exact terms and conditions under which I will perform, and I know where he is and what he's thinking at all times.

FOUR

COUNT
VON BLITZSTEIN

When Elvis Presley first came gyrating into every living room on *The Ed Sullivan Show,* few could ignore him. And, when perspiring fans made him an overnight singing sensation, not to mention an instant millionaire, I think most guys asked themselves the same question: "Now what has that kid got that turns on all the girls?"

Despite Presley's very real talents, his success introduced a period of gimmickry—singers who can't sing and musicians who can't play but who sell records in the millions anyway. I felt the need to spoof what I sensed at that time was a noisy, antimelodic trend in the music business.

But what gimmick could I offer? For a size 42 long, any overt physical flexing was out and I could no longer pass for a teen-ager. However, on the plus side of the talent

ledger, I sang off-key and played bad piano. So I decided
to make myself an illusory singer whom everybody would
want to get next to and whose talents nobody could challenge—a person of royal blood.

Thus "Count von Blitzstein" was born. I thought the
name suggested the ready romance of Old World charm
and culture. There was something magnetic in the idea
that some people are the beneficiaries of wealth and position, who haven't done anything to qualify except to be
born. Everybody likes to identify with such a fortunate
soul.

I decided to enlist the aid of my good friend George
Wayne, an actor and artist. So I stopped by his apartment, where I found him bending over some new draw-
ings for his art portfolio on his makeshift desk, an old
grocery display shelf. He had scavenged most of his furniture from the street, where it had been left for garbage
disposal. Orange crates artistically painted were stacked
against the wall in an interesting fashion, and they held
his belongings. But not much could be done with the
bathtub that sat in the middle of the room. George kept
his dirty dishes in it. Because George had no patience for
washing dishes, he let the dirty ones pile up, buying new
ones at the five and dime.

George was glad to find diversion from his portfolio and
he welcomed the opportunity to work for Count von
Blitzstein. With great zeal he approached his drawing
board and soon had sketched portraits of some members
of the Blitzstein lineage: a fierce monocled Lord von Blitzstein whose lower face was hidden by a bushy beard with
only a few strands on the top of his head. Beneath the
garlanded portrait was his birth date, "1860." And there

was a profile of the bearded King von Blitzstein with his date of birth, "1847," underneath.

I pointed out to George that by omitting a deceased date he was going to make these old codgers over a hundred years old. But George was fond of sewing clues into the pretense, a tip-off to those who would bother to appraise it with a little common sense. For my lectures that spoofed advertising he took particular relish in making graphs in which the percentages didn't add up to one hundred. Or in a chart involving a year's progress report, month by month, he would deliberately leave out a month or add a new one—"Distemper" and "Remember" were his favorites—between September and October. On the many occasions I've used these visuals, nobody ever pointed out these discrepancies.

Next we needed stationery for the Count. George affixed the Blitzstein ancestors to the top of some plain writing paper and sketched a likeness of the family castle between them with an underlining caption: "Schweinhorst Chateau, 1462–1923." He added a swag at the top of the castle with the legend, "497 years of courage." And at the bottom of the Count's stationery he lettered in script: "Addressez-vous à—507 Fifth Avenue." This was my New York address for mail and telephone messages.

The Count's first letter appeared on this letterhead. I photo-offset several hundred copies of it written in George's elaborate Old World handwriting. Count von Blitzstein announced he was ready for the world to make him a singing star and was entrusting his musical career to his New York representative, Bruce Spencer. Along with the Count's letter I mailed out a press release to the major record companies:

FOR IMMEDIATE RELEASE:

Count von Blitzstein, international playboy skier and singer par excellence, has arrived in the United States from Switzerland to pursue a singing career. The Count, born at Uskub Bosnia-Herzegovina, distinguished himself during World War II by single-handedly capturing a battalion of Bessarabians in the Carpathian Mountains.

No stranger to cloak and dagger methods, the Count experienced one spine-chilling escapade after another, finally leading a lone guerilla movement in the Antarctic until he was wounded by a stalagmite.

After the war, Count von Blitzstein was decorated for heroism by the Queen and he returned triumphantly to his ancestral seat at Uskub to continue his studies on the violoncello under the late Professor Kurzmeir, who recently committed suicide.

Music remains the Count's first love—over fast cars, fox hunts and state balls. From his mother he inherited a voice and the courage to carry on against all odds. It was Mother Blitzstein who made headlines when she was stoned while singing at a soirée for the Queen.

At Kurzmeir's suggestion, Count von Blitzstein decided to lay down the violoncello, unbuckle his sword and give up partying and hunting to bring a thrilling voice to the world; a voice that had once commanded the Queen's own Bengal Lancers, summoned the Home Guard during the great Beer Riots of 1937, shattered glassware for miles and warmed the waters of the Grand Canal as he practiced nightly, a cappella.

This, then, is Count von Blitzstein. His first conquest in the States will be an exclusive recording contract for his unique "pop" voice. All record companies are invited to bid for his services. Contact: Bruce Spencer, 507 Fifth Avenue N.Y.C.

This first mailing went to twenty-five record companies. Each envelope was sealed with a sticky red waxlike substance that George cooked on his hot plate, the recipe for which he refused to reveal even to me. He felt it gave each letter just the right touch of royal class.

I had no specific plans for this character, and no notion where it would go. The fun lay in improvising as I went along. Therefore, I was genuinely surprised at the results of the mailing. Within forty-eight hours I received telephone calls or telegrams from RCA Victor, Columbia, M-G-M, Capitol, Mercury, Liberty, London and Dot Records. Their artist and repertory producers all wanted a sample of the Count's voice. As soon as possible.

I immediately decided to record the song "Perfidia" because it was a well-known standard tune and I could handle the piano accompaniment without playing in the cracks too often. After practicing a bit in my apartment with a tape recorder, I called George and he came over to assist me in making the master tape in the living room.

Using a sound effects recording of a chattering night club audience in the background, I began to sing in a monotone, "To you, my heart cries out perfidia . . ." while accompanying myself on the piano. It was a style that my wife described this way: "If Frankenstein's monster could sing and play the piano, he'd be doing an imitation of you."

George put on his French accent and played the night club's head waiter pleading in the foreground, "Please monsieur, think of the customers eating their food! Come back tomorrow . . . you're ruining my business! I beg of you, monsieur, *fermez la bouche!*"

For the flip side, in the event a record was going to evolve from this madness, I practiced my scales—badly of course—as George spoke with an English accent pretending to be my valet:

Begging your pardon, Your Grace. Your bath has been drawn. Item two, Sire; the water in the moat has to be changed. I expect the plumber at half-past three. Lady Bottomlee rang you up and said she'd be five minutes late for the fox hunt. I've advised the kennels to hold the dogs another five minutes. With your permission, Your Grace, the barber is here. Careful, barber, that you do not shear his Lordship's curls. I have written your introduction to the Earl's dinner for Your Grace. The west wing is drafty due to a bomb which arrived in the mail and exploded prematurely against the wall. The plasterers will be here tomorrow. The drawbridge is not functioning, Your Grace, so you will have to join the fox hunt by way of the south moat. I've arranged for a raft to meet you under the tower; we will lower you by rope. For your piano recital I've invited only your relatives, as you requested, and I shall review the concert for public announcement to the peasants. Your presence has been requested at the Ostrich Races at Devonshire. Your arch supports arrived from the states; also, ah hum—the book in the plain wrapper. Baron Dusseldorf has refused your challenge to duel. Sir Thomas and his massed pipers are outside waiting to audition. You have a cable from the Earl of Wickersham, but there was no message. I've ordered the elephant-hide seat covers for your Mercedes-Benz. Colonel Boulanger of the Belgian Underground Balloon Corps requests permission to quarter his troops here next month. I have refused in your name. Begging your leave, Sire, I must withdraw to put your watch back together.

George's accent was superb, probably because he had been practicing over the previous year on his part-time job as a market researcher. He had applied for the position dressed as an Englishman, complete with accent, to make a better impression on the president of the company, who was personally interviewing applicants. And when he was hired, he was too embarrassed to drop the role.

At the time—the summer of 1958—I had eighty-five dollars left in my bank account and I blew it all to press up a hundred sample copies of 45-rpm disks displaying Count von Blitzstein's voice. I sent them around to the record companies, New York radio stations and *Billboard* music magazine. Again the reaction was immediate. Record companies began bidding furiously for the purchase of the master and one man called from Cleveland to offer ten thousand dollars. I was sympathetic to his telephone pitch —he said he was just starting a small company and needed a hit to begin with—since I once struggled with my own record company. Because he was so optimistic and a bit crazy, I thought—the offer was really too extravagant—I refused.

While I began negotiating with the record companies, I was also busy with the talent agencies who heard about the Count and wanted to handle him. Music Corporation of America, through one of its agents, Bobby Brenner, offered an appearance on *The Ed Sullivan Show* if Count von Blitzstein would sign with them. But, as the Count's personal manager, I had a healthy suspicion of talent agencies—no matter how large they were or how big their promises.

As the "Perfidia" promotion disks on my A-BELL Label began to get air plays on New York radio stations, the negotiations for the sale of the master became frantic. I found myself running around all over the city meeting first with Mitch Miller of Columbia Records, then Herman Diaz at RCA Victor, back to the office for long-distance calls from the coast, Randy Wood of Dot Records on one phone, Al Bennett of Liberty on the other. It was all quite maddening. As if somebody had thrown a pound of catnip in the middle of an orderly cat show!

Then, trouble began to loom from an unexpected source. Murray Deutsch, professional manager of Peer International, publishers of "Perfidia," was not pleased with the rendition of his song. He felt I was making fun of one of their most popular standards in such a way as to diminish its catalog standing. Deutsch threatened to take legal steps to have my recording quashed if I didn't pull it off the market. I refused, claiming he had issued a license, signed it and everything was in order. There was nothing in the license that said *how* the song was to be performed; only an agreement for me to pay the publisher two cents for every record sold.

Deutsch consulted his lawyers on a Friday but called them off the following Monday when the *Billboard* record-reviewing staff picked Count von Blitzstein as "The Novelty Record of the Week." The review said in part:

> The Count has a very amusing offering with this take-off on the old standard. It deals with a cat who is playing the piano in a French restaurant—much to the displeasure of the other customers and to the dismay of a waiter who keeps begging him to stop. The side ends on a very sour note after all the customers have been driven away. Good disk jockey item. Flip side is "Count von Blitzstein Practices the Piano."

I couldn't help musing how curious it was to be singled out as a "novelty pick" when the popular tunes on that same page were "The Bird on My Head" by David Seville doing a Donald Duck voice and other strange titles like "Hootchy-Koo" and "Itchy Twitchy Feeling."

Now the record company bidding began in earnest because this particular *Billboard* spotlight on "Perfidia" meant money in the bank. I saw RCA's man, Herman Diaz, and he offered five hundred dollars in advance against a substantial royalty arrangement. Within an hour Mercury bid a thousand dollars. By early afternoon I was so tired of all the phone calls and meetings I decided to settle with Dot Records for fifteen hundred dollars plus a percentage of the sales. Actually I was less interested in the advance money than getting it on the national market in a hurry to take advantage of the publicity. Dot's president, Randy Wood, promised to have Count von Blitzstein's voice available in record stores within a week or ten days.

To demonstrate his enthusiasm for their latest acquisition, Wood suggested I personally fly the master tape to their pressing plant in Indianapolis. He also wanted to run a full-page ad in *Billboard* with the Count's picture. Here, George's imagination prevailed as he drew a portrait of the Count, using me as the model. Incorporating some of my own features, he added an intricate beard, dashing mustache and a monocle. The haughty figure that took shape was dressed in a cutaway, sash across the chest with a gaudy medal on it, and a medallion hanging from the neck. The Count came to life as the personification of snobbish royalty—except for a cigar, which George playfully drew in his hand.

The night before I was going to Indianapolis, George had the finished artwork ready, but it was due in *Billboard's* Cincinnati office no later than noon the next day. There was only one way to meet this deadline without actually making the trip. We jumped in a cab and went to La Guardia, where I surveyed the men who were taking the midnight flight to Cincinnati. There was one face that looked especially honest; I approached the man apprehensively with my problem. Would he take the original and only copy of artwork and deliver it directly to the *Billboard* offices? I could hardly believe my ears. This gentleman not only refused money for his service but insisted he do it simply because it needed doing. I knew at that moment what it must have been like to meet the Lone Ranger.

I delivered the master tape, the ad appeared in *Billboard,* and various columnists and trade papers began praising the record with such comments as: "A disk tailored to the novelty market"—"Great for the screwball set"—"a zany spoof"—"A winner for the playful platter spinners with a wonderfully gruesome voice"—"The Count's object is ostensibly a satire of the disasters dreamed up daily on Tin Pan Alley."

Then *Billboard* bred optimism in the potential of this record with a front-page story headed: "Phantom Count, Creepy Voice—sleeper disk." And copy that began: "In New York, a phantom Eastside society figure known as Count von Blitzstein, and 'Excellency' to his social friends, is the latest phenomenon of this crazy business. . . ."

People inside the industry speculated on the Count's real identity, figuring no singer would risk his career by burlesquing the business. Everybody waited for the record to show up on the charts in trade magazines that clocked best sellers. But nothing happened. Although "Perfidia" was being played by disk jockeys—Rolfe Peterson in Salt Lake City adopted it as his daily theme song—the public didn't rush out to buy. Even MCA stopped calling when they realized the record was not selling.

Two months later the Count was dead as a doornail. Six months later I received his one and only royalty check; it was a large yellow one, decorated with elaborate printing and some fancy artwork—so attractive I couldn't bring myself to cash it. The check is framed and hangs on the wall beside my piano, a testimonial to Count von Blitzstein's brief but exciting life. The sum—18¢.

FIVE

THE
YETTA BRONSTEIN
HOAX

During the early part of 1964 while I was broadcasting a live talk show nightly from the Chicago Playboy Club, Jeanne would call in on the air from our apartment as "Mrs. Yetta Bronstein," independent candidate for President of the United States. In her Jewish dialect, she promised to establish national bingo, self-fluoridation, hang a suggestion box on the White House fence, and print a nude picture of Jane Fonda on postage stamps "to ease the post office deficit and also give a little pleasure for six cents to those who can't afford *Playboy* magazine."

Back in New York, following my stint with Playboy, I decided to find out if America was ready for a Jewish mother in the White House. I printed up several thousand political leaflets as handouts that proposed Mrs. Yetta

Bronstein on "The Best Party" ticket with a campaign slogan to fit: "Vote for Yetta and Watch Things Get Better."

In addition to leaving leaflets on airline ticket counters, in bus stations and subways and on restaurant tables—creating extensive word-of-mouth publicity—I occasionally sent out a press release from "The Best Party Headquarters" to announce Mrs. Bronstein's latest political promises. Such things as:

1. Staffing her cabinet with people who have failed in life and learned to live with it.
2. Lowering the voting age to eighteen to take juvenile delinquents off the streets and give them something to do.
3. Seizing the Russians' baggage—like the hotels in Miami—if they didn't pay their bill at the UN.

And there was always a final quote from Yetta herself: "A little sneaky my platform maybe is, but this is the kind of ingenuity I would bring to the White House as your President."

Inquiring reporters would seek out the location of "The Best Party" office at 507 Fifth Avenue in New York. The lobby directory listed it as Room 303 on the third floor; however, no matter what time of day reporters knocked on that door, or waited around, nobody was ever in—because that door led to a storage closet, always kept locked by the managing agent. I had persuaded him to rent me the door for $5 a month, including a little space inside. The sign I posted on the door announced: NATIONAL HEADQUARTERS FOR THE BEST PARTY. MRS. YETTA BRONSTEIN, CANDIDATE FOR PRESIDENT OF THE UNITED STATES OF AMERICA. In smaller print a notice read: Interviews by Appointment Only.

I had employed this same ruse for S.I.N.A., the Society for Indecency to Naked Animals, five years earlier with a broom closet door farther down the hall. Apparently, a whole new generation of reporters were falling prey to my Yetta Bronstein spoof. Just like the reporters who covered S.I.N.A., they would shove their business cards or a note under the door and ask Yetta to call them as soon as possible.

Every few days I retrieved the messages. Then Jeanne would don her dialect and call back, explaining, "Listen, Mr. Reporter, I'm very busy washing my hair so I can't talk politics in person. Also, I have a sore right thumb from shaking hands with voters. But you should know I'm for more sex and education, a cat in every meat market and a federal guarantee that there are sixteen ounces absolutely in every pound."

Jeanne could do many dialects convincingly and we put these to good use by renting a tape recording machine from the phone company and placing it in the closet with a number listed in the Manhattan directory under Yetta Bronstein's name. Each week Jeanne would record a silly message in a different voice. First was Yetta, of course, who said:

"So why are you calling me? Isn't there something better you have to do? I'm sorry I can't be here personally to answer your questions. What would the voters think if they knew I didn't do nothing but sit here on the telephone all the time? So why am I running for President? Well, one day I was doing the dinner dishes and I decided I was tired of watching TV—trying to decide which deodorant lasts longer or which cleanser is better—I wanted to do something important. So I'm running! Vote for me. Even if you don't like me. You might change your mind later on. So let me go now. I got lots of solutions to make up. I am a recording."

The next voice Jeanne recorded was that of Cynthia Lansing York, an escapee from a senior citizens' village who wanted to make it on her own. She spoke in a quivering voice:

"Hello there. Yes, I too am voting for Mrs. Yetta Bronstein. Why? Well, let me see. I knew a minute ago. Oh yes. Because she's a woman and I'm a woman and if you're a woman you'd better vote for her. We've got to stick together. Let me leave you with one of my poems called 'The City': 'Despite police, fast transit and the pill; it's not safe living in the city. For if the muggers don't get you, the air pollution will.' Good-by."

Another popular voice she recorded was Sibil Rittenhouse, Jr., a debutante who came out, got scared and went back in. This caricature of a society matron, Jeanne rather sang than spoke:

"Ta ta again. It's me, Sibil, just back from Tuxedo Park and packing my bag for a party in Rome. But before I leave, let me urge all of you to vote for Yetta Bronstein—whether you ride a Rolls-Royce or the subway. She's a charming woman with plenty of oomph. Stay in touch, won't you? And good-by Ramon, wherever you are, darling!"

Numerous organizations, clubs and college groups began requesting Yetta to speak. However, as an attractive twenty-eight-year-old blonde ingenue type, Jeanne looked more like Eva Marie Saint than Molly Picon. So I usually showed up for Mrs. Bronstein's speaking engagements, explaining Yetta was home in bed with swollen ankles. And to sustain the image of a fifty-year-old woman with shop-

ping bags and falling stockings, I would play a tape recording of Yetta singing her campaign song to the tune
of "When the Saints Go Marching In:"

> Vote Bronstein in . . .
> Vote Bronstein in . . .
> Get Bronstein into the White House
> She wants to run . . . for number one . . .
> In the Capitol . . . Washington.

> There'll be a change . . .
> There'll be a change . . .
> There'll be a change in government . . .
> When Yetta gets to be the First Lady . . .
> And also President.

Her slightly off-key rendition was hilarious and this
always helped establish an immediate rapport with the
audience. One political rally I organized at Johns Hopkins University drew a larger turnout than either George
Wallace or Richard Nixon had the week before. And
when I promised to donate Yetta's body to their medical
school someday in the name of science, the students went
wild with laughter and cheers: "We want Yetta's body!"

Next day in the Baltimore *Sun,* reporter Gerald Clarke
said: "Yetta's campaign manager admits she doesn't know
anything about the Common Market and she's not too
clear about what's going on in Vietnam. However, if
elected she will have the Government print up a little
pamphlet to explain it to her and everybody else."

Primarily by word of mouth, news about the loquacious
lady from The Bronx who wanted to be President spread
across the country, even overseas to London's *Financial
Times.* Newspapers, radio and television in the United
States and Canada began to report her campaign platform.

During the 1964 Democratic National Convention in

Atlantic City, I drove down for the day with four college student friends who were avid Bronstein supporters. Jim Freedman and Caleb Deschanel were editors of the *Newsletter,* the campus newspaper at Johns Hopkins, and Mimi Stark and Linda Sampson were students at New York University. We had rented a convertible and then pasted Yetta's homemade banners, bunting and signs all over the car. It was a real traffic stopper on the New Jersey Turnpike.

Atlantic City was a madhouse of frenzied vacationers and thousands of delegates and their families jammed into every conceivable nook and cranny. It took us nearly an hour just to find a parking space. Finally, we were lucky to park in a lot just opposite the Pageant Motel, where Lyndon Johnson and his entourage were staying, only a stone's throw from Convention Hall, where all the action was. Actually the excitement was out on the boardwalk in front of the auditorium, where the pickets were.

The five of us set up a line of march with our signs that read: YB+LBJ=YBLBJ Put a Mother in the White House! Yetta Is Tough, Shrewd and Clever. Yetta Bronstein for President.

It wasn't long before we were surrounded by people—delegates, kibitzers, reporters and state troopers. Everybody wanted literature and we gave it to them as fast as we could pull it out of our shopping bags. There was a trunk load in the car too and we made many trips before the afternoon was over. I gave several impassioned speeches that drew crowds and so disturbed the other marchers—namely George Lincoln Rockwell's followers and a dozen men in black suits with Lester Maddox, all carrying ax handles—the state troopers asked me not to speak and gave us a chalk marking on the boardwalk to follow. We tread this line up and down in front of Convention Hall, the brown-uniformed American Nazis marching rigidly on our left, displaying the swastika; the Lester Maddox people striding mutely on our right.

Several times I was challenged by two large women carrying beach bags and wearing fright wigs. One of the women who weighed at least two hundred pounds pointed a huge finger at me and shouted, "Who is this Yetta Bronstein? I never heard of her, what right does she have to run for President?"

"What right do you have to ask about her rights?" I answered. "Where do you get such a right? Shame on you! Asking such a question about one of your fellow females who may someday be your First Lady, President and Commander-in-Chief all rolled into one."

I gave her some literature, including these two open letters addressed to the President and Barry Goldwater:

Dear President Johnston:

If you want me for a V.P. to you I would be willing to step down from my campaign as President of the United States in 1964. Just think of all the votes we could swing running together.

Your family I have not met but they are wonderful people. And I love the way you ride a horse. We could all get along very well.

Meantime, if you have already someone in mind for your V.P. then I will continue to be an independent platform. You should know I have invited Mr. Goldwater to debate me. Although my people are in his background I must still consider him the enemy.

Maybe I'll see you on the beach in Atlantic City. That's my home stomping grounds and I'll be happy to show you around. I can also get many things there for you wholesale.

Well, Mr. President, whatever you decide I understand that's politics.

Hopefully,
Mrs. Yetta Bronstein

Dear Mr. Goldwater:

I, Yetta Bronstein, independent candidate for President, challenge you to a personal debate anywhere, anytime and on any subject.

Your recent concern for the safety of American women at night is good for lots of votes. I too was once chased many years ago. Women do need protection from men and for this I salute you.

But I want you should argue with me on politics. Would you do me the pleasure, Mr. Goldwater? I always enjoy a good fight and especially with one of my own people.

In conclusion, you should know I have offered myself to President Johnson for V.P. if he wants me. There's nothing wrong with playing second fiddle if everybody else plays the right tune. You know what I mean?

If Mr. Johnson chooses his own running mate like you did, then I'll ride alone. Remember my motto: "Vote for Yetta and things will get better."

Your competitor,
Mrs. Yetta Bronstein

Now the heavyset woman began to holler at me for the obvious error of spelling President Johnson's name with a "t."

"So we have a cheap printer," I explained. "What do you expect Yetta to do before she becomes President, spend all her money and go bankrupt before she can tap the Treasury?"

"Why aren't there more Bronstein supporters with you?" asked this woman's friend.

"They are here, everywhere in disguise. See those people sitting on the beach with the umbrella, and that group over there eating hot dogs, and those ladies in the smart furs? They are all rooting for Yetta."

"But we never heard of this Bronstein person before. I still think she has a lot of nerve to want to be President."

"This country was built on nerve, madam. Look at Lewis and Clark, Eli Whitney or George Washington—all great men of destiny. Mrs. Bronstein has some of their ideas."

"How could we be sure she would be a good President if we gave her our votes?"

"Would you question the solemn promise of a woman, especially a mother?" I asked.

"Never!" they shouted in unison.

A reporter from Associated Press joined me and asked, "What has Mrs. Bronstein to say on our foreign policy?"

"She says we should have one," I answered as another woman poked her way over to me. She was rather stout, wearing red shorts and a straw hat. Her question:

"Does Mrs. Bronstein wear a wig?"

"No, never. Mrs. Bronstein has nothing against wigs. It's just that she has a full head of hair."

"Where's Yetta? Where's Yetta?" a woman cried as she made her way through the crowd toward me. She was in her fifties, attractive, out of breath from running and very excited.

"I'm her campaign manager, can I help you?"

"I've got to find Yetta," she insisted.

"Well, she isn't here and I don't know where she is."

"All right then, tell her to contact me immediately. My name is *Yetta Bronstein!*"

I looked at her incredulously. She did resemble the happy-go-lucky motherly type woman Jeanne and I imagined Yetta Bronstein to be. As a matter of fact, we were thinking of casting such a person to front our campaign as Yetta, in much the same way I had selected actor-writer Buck Henry to pose as G. Clifford Prout, President of S.I.N.A. Frances Kessler, a friend and violinist at the Radio City Music Hall in Rockefeller Center, was a perfect choice for the role. But she had graciously declined, feeling it might cause a conflict of interest; Frances explained that, indirectly, she was working for Nelson B. Rockefeller, a Republican.

"You're not Yetta Bronstein!" I shouted. "You're an impostor! I know Yetta like I do my own wife . . ."

"Wait a minute! Wait a minute!" she interrupted. "I have identification, here. See, my driver's license, my Weight Watchers card, it's really me, Yetta Bronstein."

And so it was. Another Yetta Bronstein, only an honest-to-goodness real one.

"Everybody thinks I'm running for President. The neighbors, friends, relatives, even my boss at the office won't believe it's not me! He called me this morning from Philadelphia where I live. I'm here on vacation. It's all so exciting. I'd like to meet Yetta and get her autograph, maybe a picture."

I promised her she would hear from the Presidential candidate herself. And Jeanne did drop her a note a few months later to explain it was just a gag; she did the same to another Yetta Bronstein who had written from Washington, D.C., with a similar problem: Everybody thought *she* was the one running for President.

The same reporter from Associated Press returned to our line of march and began chewing me out. He had written a straight story on Yetta Bronstein that went out over the wires and then learned in the interim that I was the notorious practical joker. He kept up his harangue as I walked the picket line designated for our group; I shouted Yetta Bronstein slogans and ignored him.

When he left me and turned his attention to the students, claiming they were going to be in deep trouble back at their schools for perpetrating a hoax, I motioned to a burly state trooper and through pantomime indicated trouble was about to erupt. The officer quietly but firmly grabbed the reporter by the seat of his pants and walked him to a ramp off the boardwalk. Funny, nobody got uptight about Lester Maddox' ax-handle wielders or the goose-stepping Nazis. But Yetta—she was a safe target.

Other reporters, some with tape recorders, came around representing newspapers from all over the country. I suggested they interview Mrs. Bronstein directly by calling an unlisted number in New York. Then I gave them our home phone, where Jeanne was standing by to perform in the Yetta dialect and explain her platform.

Around 6 P.M. we went back to our car, tired and hungry but feeling good for having injected some humor into the otherwise stodgy Democratic Convention. William F. Buckley, Jr., was standing by the convertible reading the wraparound signs and I couldn't believe my eyes. He was actually smiling!

"Here you are, sir." I said, handing him a leaflet. "Please vote for Mrs. Bronstein. She's a write-in candidate and we need all the support we can get."

Buckley's smile quickly faded into a vacant, cynical look as he took the literature and walked away. I noticed he was being watched by small groups of well-dressed young men with crew cuts standing on little balconies that jutted out from the Pageant Motel across the street. Some of them came down at that time and requested literature while we rested in the car. From the bulges under their jackets I suspected they were Secret Service men.

When I called Jeanne to see how things were going from her end I learned that a flock of reporters and photographers were camped outside our apartment door, causing a slight commotion in the building lobby since we live on the ground floor. Somehow they had traced our home address, in spite of the unlisted telephone number that is supposed to be confidential information, and were all facing deadlines. Jeanne kept telling them Yetta Bronstein wasn't home and they kept insisting she was, otherwise why did she still answer the phone!

Jeanne was in a real quandary. She had to answer the phone as Yetta in order to keep the political spoof alive. And we never anticipated having to meet the press on our doorstep. Nevertheless, she carried on in the true spirit of a loyal hoaxer's wife, with the radio up loud, talking to reporters on the phone in dialect and then running to the front door as Mrs. Abel to try to calm the newsmen arriving in ever increasing numbers.

While she was on the phone with Theo Wilson of the New York *Daily News* somebody began kicking at the front door, obviously miffed at being given the runaround. That's when Jeanne read them the riot act: "Gentlemen, you are trespassing on the doorstep of *my* apartment and I will give you all exactly one minute in which to vanish!" They grumbled a little, gathered up their gear and left.

This particular "brush-off" didn't seem to clue these reporters that there was no Yetta Bronstein; rather, it convinced them more than ever that Mrs. Bronstein must be hiding in our apartment! Otherwise I don't believe their editors would have permitted the stories that appeared in the newspapers, on radio and television—concerning Mrs. Bronstein's campaign—without some sort of a disclaimer that it was a leg-puller. Granted, a few knew and didn't care, or perhaps didn't want to know, but most news people take their jobs seriously and don't fool around. Especially when it comes to political reporting.

When I arrived home late that night Jeanne reported hearing Robert Trout and Roger Mudd discuss the "Bronstein for President" platform on the CBS-TV news as did David Brinkley over the full NBC television network. There was also a letter waiting for me from Sam Brightman, chairman of the Democratic National Committee; he turned down my request for press credentials to Convention Hall, claiming there would be no story for me in Atlantic City.

On the contrary, our efforts in one day found prominence in most of the nation's dailies. Alfred Friendly, managing editor of *The Washington Post,* was apparently upset by Yetta when he began his article, "For the ultimate in revolting taste, we offer the alleged campaign of a 48-year-old Bronx housewife, Mrs. Yetta Bronstein. . . ."

The Newark *Star-Ledger* gave Mrs. Bronstein a banner headline on page one ("Watch Things Get Betta with Yetta") and a feature story by Jerry Izenberg that said in part:

> . . . the first sign of trouble for Yetta Bronstein's party came shortly after noon. Her campaign manager was told to take his sign and his four workers and move about 50 feet down the boardwalk. "I'm sorry," the state cop said, "but you will

have to move. They (the Nazis) have so many people that we just have to push you down a little to keep the traffic moving."

The *Star-Ledger* syndicated Izenberg's feature article around the country to other newspapers in its chain and *The National Observer* carried a story on Yetta under the headline "How the Little Parties Can Pull a Lot of Weight." A reporter for the Denver *Post* headed his interview: "Bronx Lady Offers to Accept VP Spot."

The Philadelphia *Daily News* ran photographs of our group on the boardwalk; and the Chicago *Daily News* Syndicate filed a series of reports to their member newspapers. James Reston covered Mrs. Bronstein's activities in Atlantic City for *The New York Times,* and Rose De Wolf, writing for the Philadelphia *Inquirer,* ended her article with: "Is Mrs. Bronstein serious? The campaign manager looked hurt. 'What kind of a question is that? Of course she's serious!' "

Motorists driving through Blairstown, New Jersey, couldn't help but notice the huge banner sign in front of one residence that read: "Yetta Bronstein slept here." Bob Hardart, a personal friend and one of the Horn & Hardart restaurant family, wanted to surprise his neighbors and passing tourists after Jeanne and I stayed over one night.

Sunday, November 1, 1964, Ben A. Franklin, writing for *The New York Times,* said:

> Mrs. Yetta Bronstein, the write-in Presidential candidate of another distinctly minority political alignment that she chooses to call The Best Party, has defined the issues in 1964 as the lack of support among her opponents for nationwide bingo and sex education in the schools. There appears to be no national consensus for bingo, and Mrs. Bronstein, a New York City housewife, may fail to carry a single precinct.
>
> Although Mrs. Bronstein didn't carry any precinct in

the election, our college friend, Jim Freedman, served as a runner for CBS News in Baltimore and he personally counted four hundred write-in-votes for Yetta from one tally alone. And in Alabama she received more write-in votes than two other heavy favorites among the voters—Arthur Godfrey and Mickey Mouse.

Our four huge scrapbooks bulged with press clippings on Yetta's unsuccessful campaign for the Presidency. *Playboy* magazine extended its regrets for her loss of our nation's highest office, saying:

> . . . Mrs. Bronstein admits that she, like Senator Goldwater, was no more than a college dropout. "But A students can be bums, while F students succeed," Mrs. Bronstein says in her defense. And to prove it she presents her 'campaigne platfform' (that's how her handouts spell it), a straightforward and hard-hitting document from which we suspect both major parties could draw a lesson for the future—from its brevity, if not from its spelling. . . .
>
> And as Mrs. Bronstein sadly concluded: "If a mother was in the White House, who would open a big mouth to her?"

We also had a few thousand letters to Yetta from fans who, according to their letters, apparently never doubted her existence. They included personal notes from well-known personalities—Carol Burnett, Jonathan Winters, Clare Booth Luce, Harry Golden, Earl Wilson, Melvin Belli, Phyllis Diller, Danny Thomas, Charles Schultz and many others.

Henry Mancini wrote Yetta, "It's people like you that make this country what it is!" During a friendly exchange of letters between Yetta and Peter Sellers, she offered him the opportunity to play her—in drag—if Hollywood ever filmed "The Yetta Bronstein Story." Mr. Sellers replied that he did not feel he could do justice to the part.

Who could resist such an outpouring of friendship from so many strangers? We couldn't. Jeanne and I decided to keep Mrs. Yetta Bronstein alive by throwing her hat into other political rings.

Using the pen name Mrs. Yetta Bronstein, Jeanne wrote "The President I Almost Was." Her agent, Bruce Spencer, sold the manuscript, first in England to publisher Peter Wolfe, then in the states to Hawthorn Books, with the paperback rights going to Avon Books.

The income from these book sales permitted the necessary finances to launch bigger and better things for Yetta, the first being to challenge John V. Lindsay for residency in New York City's Gracie Mansion.

SIX

YETTA BRONSTEIN VERSUS JOHN V. LINDSAY

FOR IMMEDIATE RELEASE

Mrs. Yetta Bronstein, former independent candidate for President of the United States in 1964, has announced she will run for Mayor of New York City on the *Best Party Ticket*.

Speaking before a group of Bronx housewives who have promised to ring doorbells for her, Mrs. Bronstein said her platform will embody the same high principles that lost her the Presidential election. Explaining her loss by a landslide, she said: "It was only because I wasn't too well known and had such a short time in politics. At least in New York City I know many thousands of people who know other thousands I don't even know."

Among Mrs. Bronstein's reforms are: one city boss, less pollution, clean subways, pigeon shelters and stronger government.

This announcement to various news desks in the summer of 1965 launched our next effort to get Yetta elected to something, anything.

Reporters took the bait and began calling—John Wingate of WOR Radio News, Ralph Blumenthal of *The New York Times,* Marlene Saunders of ABC-TV News— eager to fill in the August drought with something light-hearted.

Jeanne had an uncanny ability not only to create a very believable Jewish dialect but also to think as Yetta Bronstein over the phone. Her razor-sharp dialogue, often under fire from hardened reporters, would stand up as a comedy routine, as these verbal calisthenics demonstrate:

REPORTER: Mrs. Bronstein, if you are elected Mayor, what will you do about the present water shortage?

YETTA: Like our grandmothers who had to go fetch and carry their water in buckets from a well, I suggest we do the same. We should line up at our neighborhood fire hydrants, ready to fill up. The water commissioner could throw the switch maybe at only certain times of the day. Carrying heavy water in buckets and dishpans would discourage us from wasting.

REPORTER: How about city finances?

YETTA: To tax or not to tax—that is the question. Some candidates say that they said that first. But it was William Shakespeare who said it first. And I don't think he knew what he was talking about either. The bosses pay Peter to pay Paul and Paul is robbing Peter, but only to put in his own pockets. Last names I won't give you. I wouldn't want to offend.

REPORTER: What are your views on crime?

YETTA: Where's the good news in the papers? All you read about is crime. It's what sells newspapers and keeps people interested. But what would happen if there was only good news? No more crime! Maybe no more newspapers. So I would ban bad news. For the people who crave depressing things and can't live without trouble, I would send them to Cuba.

REPORTER: What about the safety of women in the streets, Mrs. Bronstein?

YETTA: I would put a purse on the market that if a snatcher comes along and takes it from you, you push a button on it. And it sets up a smoke screen. If the robber gets away he leaves a trail behind him. And the police can follow if they aren't busy towing away cars. Even if the thief gets away completely with the money, you have the satisfaction of knowing that his sinuses are ruined.

REPORTER: Do you have a solution for the traffic problem?

YETTA: I would ban all cars from Manhattan. Instead, I would have New Jersey made into a parking lot. What they got is better?

REPORTER: Mrs. Bronstein, what is your opinion of the other candidates? First, Mr. Beame.

YETTA: Who ever heard of him before he decided to run for Mayor?

REPORTER: And Mr. Lindsay.

YETTA: He's very good-looking. A beauty queen I'm not, but I discovered that looks alone don't make the person. I would love to meet Mr. Lindsay, if that sweet man would like to debate with me. Anytime, anywhere.

REPORTER: And Mr. Buckley?

YETTA: Well, I've seen Mr. Buckley on TV and I've read

his magazine in my doctor's office. I think he should
go into show business. He'd be so much better as an
actor on Peyton Place.

REPORTER: What is your general philosophy, Mrs. Bronstein?

YETTA: I say it's time to get the bosses out of Gracie Mansion and put a Mother in there. New York needs a
Mother! That's me, a Mother. So vote for me, O.K.
I'll give you low rent, plenty of hot water and occa-
sional taxes. Mr. Lindsay is handsome, Mr. Buckley
is smart and Mr. Beame is also running. But *I* am a
natural born leader.

For beeper telephone interviews on the air Jeanne had
a pitch pipe handy and would tune up for an *a cappella*
version of her campaign song, also in dialect:

"And now, I'd like to sing my victory song. It's to the
tune of 'Home on the Range,' and I'd like to invite the
listening audience to hum along, if you know how:

>Oh, give her a home
>Where the bosses now roam
>And the bookies are
>Free to make hay.
>Where seldom is heard
>A discouraging word
>About graft until election day.

>Home, home on the range
>Let Yetta be cook for a change.
>So vote Bronstein in,
>End the strife, crime and sin,
>And Man-hat-tan will be gay again."

The water shortage was still acute in New York, and
city officials announced they were sending several engi-

neers to California for a consultation with professional
rainmakers. Yetta responded with an open letter to the
citizens:

> I am very upset over the present plan to send officials to ·
> California where they will watch the rainmakers try to
> squeeze the clouds with their bag of tricks. Why don't the
> politicians go to Arizona and learn a few rain dances from
> the Indians also? I intend to fire any person in my adminis-
> tration who uses voodoo or other forms of witchcraft to
> play magic tricks on the pocketbooks of the people!

One of our mailings that found its way on numerous
advertising agency bulletin boards was this particular announcement:

> Mrs. Yetta Bronstein, independent candidate for Mayor,
> requested a new advertising agency to handle her campaign.
> She said: "In 1964 I didn't know too much about my image
> and how it could help me lose the Presidential election.
> That's why I said 'yes' to the first advertising agency that
> came along looking for some new business. They were will-
> ing to handle my account on a 10 per cent commission fee,
> so what could I lose?
>
> "Then I find out these ad people were as green about
> politics as I was. If they had told me in the first place their
> major accounts were pots, pans, overalls, hearing aids and
> toothpicks, I would have taken another agency that wanted
> to handle me. At least they advertised a race track and were
> familiar with winners!
>
> "This time I want an agency that knows how to charm
> the public into buying anything. You won't get rich but
> you'll have fun and I'm easy to work with.
>
> "All major advertising agencies are invited to make
> their presentations by mail to show what they can do for
> the next woman Mayor of New York City."

Much to my disappointment, not a single agency responded. So it was onward and upward with a new piece of propaganda:

$50 REWARD

For information leading to the whereabouts of Mrs. Yetta Bronstein, independent candidate for Mayor of New York City. Mrs. Bronstein was last seen speaking on the corner of 42nd St. and Fifth Ave. about politics. She was wearing a red, white and blue dress and shouting campaign slogans through a megaphone that once belonged to Rudy Vallee. If you have any news at all, day or night, please call YU 6-0717. *Informants will be protected. No questions asked.* NOTE: This circular has been paid for by the CITIZENS FOR THE SAFE RETURN OF MRS. YETTA BRONSTEIN

This leaflet was left all over Manhattan, and our storage closet telephone rang around the clock. Those callers fortunate enough not to get a busy signal heard Yetta herself on tape:

Hello, I'm back! I've been found! Thank you for worrying about me. A nice sanitation truck man picked me up when he saw me in the Bronx Zoo. I was watching the orangutans. And they were watching me. The day slipped by and I was reported missing. . . . But don't you forget to vote me in as your next Mayor. O.K.? This is Yetta Bronstein signing off to go home and make dinner.

A few days of this nonsense and we were forced to erase the tape to prevent the telephone from being jammed with an overload of incoming calls.

As the race for Mayor approached the zero hour for Buckley, Beame, Lindsay and Bronstein, I decided to stage one final grandstand play on the Friday before the Tuesday election. This would be a mobile campaign around Manhattan with a Dixieland band, banners, followers, speeches and leaflets.

First I had to obtain a police permit and I soon learned this was no easy task. Although the cost of the permit was only five dollars, the officer in charge of permits at the Seventeenth Precinct told me it was going to take a few days, maybe longer. This was on the Monday before our Friday parade.

I returned each day to the station house and was stalled for various reasons: ". . . the matter is still being considered; the request has to go through channels; we can't be sure of its approval; these things take time."

By Thursday I still didn't have the necessary permit, and Jeanne was becoming a little nervous. We had already hired the band, a convertible—when the Hertz rental agent said they were all out of convertibles, I mentioned confidentially it was for a mayoral candidate; he found one in ten minutes—the signs were painted, ten thousand pieces of literature were printed, and a dozen friends and fans were prepared to shout and sing for Yetta. But we needed that permit or the cops would slap us with a summons every five minutes. The latest word from the sergeant was to return the next day, Friday, an hour before we began.

This was playing it too close for comfort. What if they refused to issue the permit? Our expenses were going to total around two hundred dollars, perhaps all for nothing.

That night I spoke to a former ward politician who lived near us and he said I should provide some money to the right people at the station house and the permit would be issued forthwith—say about fifty dollars for "expenses."

I refused to go along with his suggestion. The very idea that New York's Finest would stoop to accepting payola was unthinkable. I would have no part of it. Nor could Jeanne accept the thought that anybody at the Seventeenth

Precinct would take money from a complete stranger. Especially when they were all on good salaries, took an oath of office to obey and administer the law and inherited a certain amount of pride that goes along with every New York City police uniform. Furthermore, if I did offer any money, in a moment of weakness, I might be arrested on the spot for bribery!

However, Jeanne felt that the police officers were going to such a lot of trouble in preparing and issuing our permit, we should do something for them if only to express our gratitude. Since it was so close to Halloween she decided to bake them a cake, complete with a sugar witch on top, decorated with orange and black icing that spelled out: "To the 17th Precinct boys from Yetta Bronstein." I seconded the motion.

The next morning, armed with this cake wrapped in cellophane, I showed up at the Seventeenth Precinct on East Fifty-first Street in the heart of Manhattan. My entourage waited outside at a discreet distance.

"This is for you and all the boys from Yetta Bronstein, your next Mayor," I announced proudly to the patrolman on duty. "I'm here to pick up Mrs. Bronstein's parade permit for today."

The shocked officer took the cake and my five dollars for the permit into a back room. He returned about five minutes later with a dozen other men in uniform and several plainclothes detectives. A sergeant, holding the cake in one hand, gave me my permit with the other. Everybody just stood around quietly looking me over. The amazed expressions on their faces and the silence were almost embarrassing.

I waved good-by and went outside to join our caravan. But I don't think I shall ever forget seeing all those tough cops disarmed by a simple little cake that cost only $1.27 to make. If ever Yetta Bronstein rose to meet a crisis, this was perhaps her finest moment.

And so we toured midtown Manhattan for most of the day, stopping on street corners to play a few tunes, answer questions from the crowds and pass out literature. Everybody wanted to meet Yetta, but they had to settle instead for her campaign manager. Our band was tagged "Yetta Bronstein's Matzo Ball Orchestra" and included members of the Radio City Music Hall Orchestra under the direction of trumpet player Norman Beatty, a long-time friend and former classmate from my hometown in Ohio. He was assisted by Jack Schnupp on trombone, John Bartlett on tuba and Norman Forrest playing the viola with his gloves on—for an added comic effect. I joined in on the snare drum when I wasn't busy talking over a bull horn about Yetta's platform.

Jeanne handled the friends and fans who passed out the materials at every stop. She also picked up a few volunteers along the way who just wanted to help out and join in the fun. I had already sent night letters to the news desks at NBC, CBS and ABC advising them of our itinerary, but it wasn't until around 3 P.M. when we were approached by a news reporting team. They were a camera crew working for Huntley-Brinkley, on orders to interview Mrs. Yetta Bronstein for the seven o'clock NBC-TV news that evening.

They waited around for half an hour and insisted on interviewing the candidate herself; Jeanne didn't want to spoil the spoof by stepping in at that point and I was unable to persuade the camera director he should settle for her campaign manager. They were disappointed and so were we.

After the NBC film crew left for another assignment, Herb Kaplow showed up with a tape recorder and I spoke to him for NBC Radio News:

". . . at that time she was running for President of the United States. Now that was a year ago and she lost. But that didn't discourage this mother. She bounced right back and is presently running for the Mayorship of New York. I ask the voters right now: what kind of a woman would you want to put in Gracie Mansion except a woman who is a two-time loser running again? Think of all the experience she'll bring to the city. . . !"

Kaplow ended with:

Although her name isn't even on the ballot, she's Yetta Bronstein who's been holding street corner rallies on her own. That was her campaign manager. The NBC news team Huntley-Brinkley will bring you radio's most comprehensive election night coverage Tuesday.

Around 4 P.M. another camera crew found us and they were from WNBC-TV News. They were disappointed because Yetta wasn't around but decided to go ahead and interview me. Robert McNeil and Les Dennis handled this assignment. Their cameraman panned around our Dixieland Band in the convertible and picked up the sign "New York Needs a Mother." Announcer Les Dennis yelled to me over the music, "Where's Yetta?" I noticed the sound man fingering his dials and listening intently through earphones while the cameraman focused on me for a closeup. It was time for a filibuster:

"Well, Yetta's supposed to be here. Last I saw her she was headed for the powder room of the Plaza. And that was two hours ago. What can I tell you? Except that she's been following our car around feeling the pulse of the people. We're already a half hour behind our schedule.

Everybody's excited. Nobody knows where she is. All I know is that we're out here getting votes for her. I can't be responsible for where she is or what she's doing. She's supposed to be here. It's a terrible state of affairs. . . ."

Les Dennis interrupted me momentarily to suggest it was unusual for a candidate to be absent from her followers on the eve of the election. I defended Yetta vigorously:

"You don't see Mr. Lindsay out, do you? But you see a few of his people. You don't see Mr. Buckley and you see *none* of his people. As for Mr. Beame, wherever he is, most of his voters are for Yetta and will probably switch in the booth. But we're out campaigning for her to make sure. We don't have to have her present, except in spirit, but I'm very disturbed that she isn't here. Now look at our huge crowd, listen to the band, notice the smiles on the musicians' faces—try to stay together, fellows, and play faster, not louder. You don't have this kind of excitement for Buckley, Lindsay or Beame. No, Mr. Dennis, this is *real* excitement."

I was now shouting at the top of my lungs as the musicians misunderstood my cue and began to play both faster and louder. Dennis too was yelling questions at me concerning Mrs. Bronstein's standing with the voters and her platform. I rambled right on:

"I think she has a chance to win only if people will wake up and decide to write her in. Generally people go with the Republicans or Democrats or Liberals. If they could decide to be different this time, not to just be a sheep, following the sheep, Yetta has a good chance. You know she has her own pollster, an uncle who used to be a lawyer. And he shows her winning hands down at this time. As to her platform? Yetta wants self-fluoridation, you know, where each person carries around his own fluoride pills and drops one in whenever he takes a drink; she feels that everybody should have an individual right under the First Amendment of the Constitution to fluoridate or not to fluoridate. And speaking of water, because New York has a drought, Yetta will give us all the water we want by letting us drink Long Island Sound. Yetta will personally man the pumps to take water from the Atlantic Ocean and divert it back into Long Island Sound. She also thinks that everybody should be free to walk the streets at night unmolested. As a woman who was once chased, she is going to be tough on muggers and robbers. You know she personally wears a karate black belt. This is the woman who will run Gracie Mansion with an iron fist, like she runs her own home."

Dennis argued that a father image would be better as Mayor.

"No," I countered. "Because women are in control of the money and make the family decisions. Also, we all look to our mothers to do the right thing. And, most important, we can resolve our guilt feelings—that we've never done right by our mothers—by putting a kind of super-mother in Gracie Mansion. As mother-mayor, Mrs. Bronstein would represent *all* our mothers by proxy."

"Thank you, Mr. Abel," said Dennis with some relief and he added, "Mrs. Bronstein also ran for President in 1964. She lost."

When the interview ended, Les Dennis looked at me as though I were stark raving mad. My costume helped a bit—red baseball cap, with a gas mask bag over my shoulder. Throughout the filming he had to hustle to get in his questions. I talked a mile a minute, running one sentence over another. This was a technique I picked up from watching professional politicians. By talking rapid-fire I prevented the film cutters from editing chunks of conversation: it was all or nothing.

And so my complete seven-minute interview was telecast that night, Friday, October 29, 1965, in prime time before millions of viewers. To advertisers, those minutes of television time represented thousands of dollars. But Yetta Bronstein—a nonexistent candidate—had made the news at an expenditure of only $201.27.

SEVEN

BRONSTEIN RUNS AGAIN

Fifth Avenue in New York is one way going south, except for parades; they are usually northbound. I don't know why this is, any more than I know why I've always wanted to march in one of the many parades that frequently besiege Fifth Avenue. When it was announced there would be a parade in honor of Israel's twentieth anniversary, I decided this would be the perfect opportunity—not only to join a parade but also to announce Yetta Bronstein's candidacy for the Presidency in 1968.

For several days I made phone calls to the Israeli ambassador's office. They were reluctant to grant permission for Mrs. Bronstein's contingent to march even though I impressed them with her outstanding qualifications—politician, author and den mother. After I had given up, I

got a call that the official O.K. had been granted, leaving
one day to line up our friends and followers.

Sunday morning, April 28, 1968, the weather was beautiful. And thousands of people turned out to view the
parade, which had already started as we arrived and tried
to find our position in the line of march. We wandered
around the staging area, admiring the colorful costumes
while bands played, batons twirled and drums rolled.

Our marchers included Arnold Lasky, an attorney, who
played drill sergeant while his wife, Susan, was our drum
majorette. Dr. Tony Shaw brought his entire family.
Larry Wolf, an actor, served as conductor. Evie and Bill
Luebkeman led their two dogs on leashes, both decently
clothed and wearing "Vote for Yetta" sandwich signs.

For music, Don Meresco, a teacher-composer, played
bass drum; I pounded a street drum; and two musicians
from Radio City Music Hall, Joe Gallo and Herb Levy,
handled violin and piccolo respectively. Bill Witt, just
out of college, played on a lone cymbal with a stick to
round out our "band."

The parade chairman motioned us to section "P." It
was the very last unit in the parade; last except for the
New York sanitation trucks that would clean up after us.
As the snappy sixty-piece drum and bugle corps in front
of us struck out in the line of march, they totally obliter-
ated our musical efforts. We soon learned to save our
music. When they paused between Sousa marches, we
would sneak in—or rather squeak in—our medley from
Fiddler on the Roof.

Jeanne whirled crepe-paper streamers. And most everybody carried signs. One mounted on a broom read: "Clean
Sweep with Yetta." Another was tacked on an up-ended
mop: "Mop Up politics with Mrs. Bronstein!"

Along the line of march people kept shouting, "Where's Yetta?" And we would yell back, "She's in the reveiwing stand with the other dignitaries. Where else?"

Some of our college friends passed out "Bronstein for President" literature along Fifth Avenue from a grocery cart festooned with flags and bunting. One of the more popular pieces heralded Yetta's plans to disband the U.S. Post Office:

> Mrs. Yetta Bronstein will disband the UNITED STATES POST OFFICE if elected President in 1968. Instead, she will breed ten million pigeons and train them to carry microfilm to replace conventional air mail. (Mrs. Bronstein is personally feeding pigeons by the hundreds in Central Park with a new bird food sex stimulant that prevents birth control.)
>
> She will also eliminate the Zip Coade * because Mrs. Bronstein feels it is useless. For her test she mailed two identical letters at the General Post Office in New York addressed to the same place only a mile away. The one *with* the Zip Code took thirty-nine hours for delivery. The one *without* the Zip Code took only twenty-six hours!
>
> In addition, she will bring back the Pony Express for all first-class mail in Manhattan. This will inject the charm of Old New York and guarantee delivery in *less than four hours.*
>
> Another part of her dynamic new mail program is to use unemployed people to deliver packages en route to the employment office for their weekly relief checks. This will not only insure speedy delivery of parcel post but also keep millions of unemployed people in good physical condition until they find jobs.
>
> All voters who support Mrs. Bronstein's program are urged to write her. She is not interested in hearing from people who disapprove.

Drum majorette Susan Lasky, who had never before

* Temporary-typist spelling error.

held a baton in her life, handled one now. She had to hold
it because she couldn't twirl it. As a running gag, every
fifty feet or so, she threw the baton up as high as she
could—the crowds watched it go up, up—then Susan would
cringe and run away as the baton fell to the pavement.
Every single time she received sympathetic "ohs" and
applause of encouragement.

In the reviewing stand at Sixty-ninth Street were such
distinguished people as Mayor John Lindsay, Senator
Jacob Javits and General Yitzhak Rabin, Israeli Ambassador to the United States. As was the custom, we stopped,
turned to face the dignitaries and honored them with a
lusty version of Yetta's campaign song—accompanied by
the five-piece band—as interpreted by our thirty or so
marchers. (We had picked up a few strangers along the
way who just wanted to join this "happening.")

We made a clumsy right face and continued our march
while the smiling dignitaries applauded politely and a
voice announced over the public address system, "That
was Mrs. Yetta Bronstein, independent candidate for
President of the United States in 1968. This is the only
political representation in the parade."

The "Bronstein for President" campaign went into high
gear when Inez Robb, nationally syndicated newspaper
columnist, devoted a feature article to Yetta based upon
one of our handouts during the Parade for Israel. She
said in part:

> As usual, Yetta's preliminary platform is succinct and to
> the point. She promises there will be no stealing, cheating
> or arguing among my government officials in Washington.
> "If politicians want to insult each other and carry on the
> way they do today, let them join the Army, Navy or
> Marines!

"I Mrs. Yetta Bronstein urge you to vote for me and help put a mother in the White House. I promise to run this great country with a strong arm, the same way I run my home.

"Now, young people of America, I would like to take you each by the hand and explain some facts of life that aren't in your school books. First, who is the only person in your life you trust? Answer: Your mother. Second, who really handles all the money in your family and makes all the important decisions. Answer: Your mother.

"Finally, if the good fairy gave you one great wish to come true, who would benefit most from such a dream? Answer: Your mother. Think of all the things your mother did for you. The feeding, changing, washing, ironing, telling bedtime stories, lying for you, crying for you—everything to make you big and strong. Now, you can pay her back by putting me in office. I will represent all your mothers and act in their behalf for you!"

To lend credence to Yetta's existence and start word-of-mouth publicity, I mailed out numerous copies of Inez Robb's column to VIPs everywhere. Mrs. Bronstein also wrote to the CIA and applied for a job as a U.S. spy ". . . for insurance in case I lose the election in 1968." E. D. Echols, director of personnel for the Central Intelligence Agency, wrote back: ". . . until we have had an opportunity to review your qualifications, we could not determine what possibilities might be available for you." But he enclosed application blanks.

A letter of inquiry to A.C. Nielsen Company, the world's largest television rating service, concerning Mrs. Bronstein's chances of winning the election, brought a personal reply from Mr. Nielsen himself:

Dear Mrs. Bronstein,
    In reply to your letter I can say only that A.C. Nielsen Company does not engage in the making of political

polls and, therefore, that we would be unable to ascertain your chances to win the presidency in 1968.

Very sincerely yours,
A.C. Nielsen, Chairman

Mrs. Bronstein contacted the United Arab Republic Tourist Office to see if it would be safe for a Jewish President to visit Cairo. The Arabs and Israelis were constantly exchanging gunfire across the Suez Canal and I wanted to protect my candidate in the event she decided to become a world traveler.

Dear Mrs. Bronstein:

In reference to your letter of June 16, 1968, we wish to assure you that the United Arab Republic welcomes all Americans regardless of race, creed, color, or religious affiliations. You will find peace and good will wherever you go in our country and you find the people most hospitable and friendly.

We are sending you under separate cover a selection of our travel literature.

Very truly yours,
M. Fouad Shadi, Director

When the Israeli newspaper *Maariv La'noar* heard about this new Arab policy, they assigned reporter Nily Grunstein to New York to write a feature story on Mrs. Bronstein's political campaign.

Yetta also wrote both Mr. Humphrey and Mr. Nixon for autographed pictures. They sent them promptly, autographed identically: "To Yetta Bronstein, with best wishes." And Mr. Humphrey added a personal note on White House stationery: "In a field that gets more crowded all the time—and as one candidate to another—I wish you good luck in your campaign."

Look magazine was the first publication to give us national publicity in an issue that featured Governor and Mrs. Nelson Rockefeller on the cover. Their "In the Know" department announced: "Mrs. Yetta Bronstein of the Bronx, N.Y. will run again this year as an independent candidate for the U.S. Presidency." There was no hint it was a gag.

To my surprise, Godfrey Cambridge commented on the NBC-TV *Today* show that he would be supporting Mrs. Bronstein. Cambridge also appeared on the *Merv Griffin Show* and said: "I finally found a little Jewish lady who is running for President of the United States. And I'm for her. So all you other politicians stop bothering me!"

Jeanne had written Godfrey a note as Yetta to thank him for the publicity and he read parts of it on the air:

> . . . my biggest fear, now that you're supporting my candidacy is that I should win! Think of it. If I were President of the United States, I'd have to dance with Charles de Gaulle. . . . I would like to offer you the Vice-Presidency; we could use a comedian in the White House. What we've got now is better? Well, Mr. Cambridge, be careful on West End Avenue where you live; there are a lot of muggers on that street. I'm signing this letter with my personal signature; it might be worth a few dollars some day if you are ever again in need. . . .

During the three weeks prior to the November election Yetta Bronstein's campaign picked up momentum. While Jeanne spent many hours on the phone talking in dialect to reporters, I was out on the street with leaflets and press releases for eager citizens. We kept expecting the bubble to burst, that Yetta would be exposed by a newspaper or magazine. But this didn't happen. So we kept priming the publicity pump with crazier copy.

An AFL-CIO union newspaper, the *RWDSU Record*,

devoted an in-depth article to "The Best Party" written by Sylvana Foa that quoted Yetta:

> I had the idea to have a kissing booth where I would sell kisses for one dollar a pucker. . . . When I was looking for a free place to hold meetings, I found opportunity at my foot doctor's office. He has a wonderful sitting room and all my friends go there an hour before my appointment so we can sit around and discuss strategy. What about the space program? Personally it makes me dizzy to watch those astronauts blast off. And then they go round and round. I can't even hold my own on a merry-go-round. And what if we should find somebody living up there—Moon people or Mars people. Here we are littering up their worlds with smashed up rockets. Suppose we look like chickens to them, and what if they like drumsticks too! Better that Congress should explore all that unfilled space inside the cereal boxes and candy wrappers and other food packages. What are we going to find on the moon anyway? A lot of rocks? You can't take a vacation there, wear a swim suit or learn to cha-cha. So what good is it to go there, plant a flag, turn right around and come back! If I'm elected President I'll go into the backyard of the White House some night, dig up a few rocks and *pretend* they came from the moon. Who's to know?

Erma Bombeck's syndicated newspaper column touched base on most of the Bronstein campaign issues. So did the New York *Daily News* with its five million circulation and a story by Dennis Eskow that concluded: "She'll have kosher delicatessen at state dinners. It sits heavy on the stomach so foreign dignitaries wouldn't stay at the White House too late and Yetta can turn off the lights earlier."

On Sunday, October 27, 1968, *The New York Times Magazine* headlined a story: "If you don't like Hubert, Dick or George, how about Lar, Yetta or Eldridge?" The author, William H. Honan, had spoken with Jeanne on the phone and she gave him one of her best performances. His story ran with a photograph of Jeanne passing out literature in New York's Bryant Park. *Times* photographer Sam Falk had taken the picture on assignment without being aware that Mrs. Bronstein was a spoof.

Honan included the highlights of Yetta's campaign and made serious references to "the candidate of the Best Party, Mrs. Yetta Bronstein, who rattles on in rich Bronx accents, her sentences ending with a rising inflection. The minor-party candidates this year comprise a hodge-podge of fractious independents including a Yippie candidate, a put-on candidate (TV comedian Pat Paulsen) and the Jewish Mother candidate."

For this *New York Times* interview Jeanne added several new ideas that found their way into Honan's article: "I'm for more sex education, but let's make it very *boring*. I'm also opposed to the war in Vietnam. I would withdraw. It won't get any better even if we win, you know."

This is a portion of the broadcast that gave Yetta Bronstein her biggest boost in the New York area. It was a telephone-talk show on radio and Jeanne fielded questions with callers in her dialect:

"I'd like to know what kind of crest you're gonna use on your coat of arms," asked a woman listener.

"I'm not sure yet," responded Yetta. "Maybe I'll have my mink dyed rabbit or something humble like that. So the masses won't ever forget that even as President I'm still one of them."

Another caller mentioned that the President has a full-time photographer on hand to record every moment of his history.

"Well, as part of my economy drive," said Yetta, "I would have my pictures taken four for twenty-five cents in the Woolworth's store near the White House."

This same caller reminded her that President Johnson was offering his memoirs for a million dollars.

"I'll take five hundred dollars," Yetta replied.

"Yetta, how do your relatives feel about your running for public office?" another voice called in on the air.

"They have all said the same thing: 'Yetta, what do you need the presidency for? You could earn more money at General Motors as their president.' But I have to tell them the truth. I'm not qualified to run General Motors."

"Who is running as your Vice-President?" asked a gruff man's voice.

"I don't have one as yet. Would you be interested?"

"Well, maybe," he said. "But after four years working under you in the White House would I be able to collect unemployment insurance?"

"I don't know," said Yetta. "But wouldn't it look a little silly for the former Vice-President of the United States to stand in line at the unemployment office waiting for his check?"

This sharp fellow suggested that the other people in line would probably recognize him and allow him to go to the head of the line.

Yetta changed the subject by pondering aloud about the laundry facilities at the White House. "Do they have to send the laundry out?" she asked the producer. He responded from the control room with a signal that he was going to dial directly to the White House and tie in the call on the air so that Yetta could find out personally.

"May I help you?" asked the White House operator.

"Yes, I wonder if Mr. Johnson happens to be in the house today."

"Which Mr. Johnson?" queried the operator.

"Which one?" exploded Yetta. "You got more than one? Hello. Hello. Talk to me, please. This is long distance and I'm paying."

"You mean President Johnson?" purred the operator sweetly.

"Yes," said Yetta.

"Yes, he is here."

"Oh, well that's fine. I'm just checking. I would like to know, could he talk to me?"

"No. I'm sorry. He's in conference," said the operator.

"Oh, I see," Yetta sighed with relief. "I'm glad he's keeping busy. I'm running for President myself and I would like to . . . hello, hello, you still there?"

"Is all this being recorded?" asked the operator suspiciously.

"No. It's alive. On the air," explained Yetta.

At this point the operator seemed to panic. She insisted that Yetta turn off her recorder and said she was going to transfer the call to the White House press office. The radio audience could hear the conversation between the operator and a press officer as the latter was told about a caller on the air with a question. The officer requested Yetta to "turn off the live because we don't like to be put on the air and there is a policy against that."

"They're chicken, aren't they?" said Yetta after the White House operator and press officer had told her to write for information and hung up.

"That *was* the White House you had on the wire?" asked the next caller.

"Of course. Would I lie to you?" said Yetta.

"They were afraid the moment they thought it was live," offered the same caller. "This is the political *coup* of the year. Fantastic! The minute they heard it was live, they said, 'Turn it off, turn it off.' I mean, it's absolutely amazing. It speaks for itself. I'm still recovering from the shock."

"Well, it's a shame," said Yetta sadly. "This is what's wrong with our country. If I were in the White House I would spill everything. No secrets in my government. The doors would come off all the offices, even the Pentagon. And it would be like a nice big happy family once again."

Another listener called in on the show to express her amazement at the brusque White House manners and commented on the fact the operator asked *"Which* Mr. Johnson?"

"Maybe he has a double," explained Yetta. "I have one. I figure I'll let *her* take the abuse, the rotten eggs, the spoiled fruit. If elected President I'll even let her run things a couple of days a week. Who will know the difference?"

A male caller added, "Well, they claim that Mao Tse-tung is doing just that. Remember the dispute when he swam the eight hundred miles down the river, or something?"

"Yes," said Yetta. "I remember the picture in *Life* magazine. His head was bobbing in the water. The Chinese were trying to prove he was really alive. Then there are also those who claim it was just a head bobbing in the water."

The final call came from a little old lady who asked

Yetta what she thought of Presidential candidate George Wallace.

After a respectful pause Yetta answered: "Well, some people say he's a nice man. But I wouldn't want to marry him."

EIGHT

THE CRAZY AD CAMPAIGN

Jay Murray, a transportation advertising executive in St. Paul and Minneapolis, was responsible for selling advertising space on a thousand Twin City buses. When I met him he disclosed his problem: sometimes he had unsold spaces on advertising racks inside the buses. These were often filled with public service announcements, such fascinating bits of information as the number of calories in a ton of rhubarb, the weather in southern Rhodesia or the weight of a pregnant elephant.

When Murray hired me to figure out some better way in which to fill those empty ad spaces, I spent several weeks riding New York buses and subways thinking about the problem. Then one day I was caught in the crush at 5 P.M. on an IRT uptown train. If you've never had that experience you've missed something, for the subway train during rush hours is like a can of worms, with people wriggling in and out at each screeching stop. Anyway, there I was trying to position my hands so the guy next to me would stop looking suspicious, like I was picking his pocket. Realizing maybe I should hold onto my own pockets, I let my arms dangle, trying to avoid nudging the lady in front so she wouldn't take me for a pervert.

I found myself trying to read the advertisements on the overhead racks past all the bobbing heads, but I saw only fragments of different ads. The effect was rather amusing: "Smokey the Bear says . . ." "Smoke Kools." "Let your fingers do the walking . . ." "And leave the driving to us." "Thom McAn Shoes . . ." "For Your Hemorrhoids" "Do You Have *Bad Breath?* . . ." You have a friend at Chase Manhattan Bank."

Thus was born my comedy concept called *Crazy Ads,* a composite of far out, zany ideas that were assembled like legitimate ads. For instance:

WANTED
Bright young man to conduct symphony orchestra. Knowledge of music helpful but not essential. Must be able to wear size 52 tuxedo. Prefer good party mixer who can dance the waltz and charm wealthy patrons with witty comments.

ARE YOU TOO MEEK OR FRIENDLY?
If people are always stepping on you, let us turn you into a raging bully! Our SCHOOL FOR AGGRESSION teaches dirty street fighting, how to write poison pen letters, 100 nasty words for everyday situations, and 20 mean ways to get revenge.

WILL THE ELDERLY GENTLEMAN
attired in footman's clothing who sat next to me on TWA Flight #43 to St. Louis, eating a liverwurst

sandwich, please contact me immediately? Important role in movie waiting for you.

BABYSITTER-DISPATCHER WANTED
Sit with babies from 9 to 5. Then sit with me from 5 to 9. Finally, dispatch trucks from 9 to midnight. Prefer mature girl with nice build, a commanding voice and some experience with the double clutch. My wife does not know about this ad.

Jay Murray's reaction to the ads was immediately enthusiastic and he arranged for half a dozen different ones to be placed on all his buses as soon as they could be printed up.

A week later the first Crazy Ads appeared and the results were electrifying. Normally irritable commuters were laughing out loud while hanging on to their straps—an unusual happening inside a public transportation vehicle! Laughter led to conversation. Soon, men were offering their seats to women; and even the drivers waited another second or two before slamming their doors on elderly ladies. A happy air prevailed within the buses as never before.

One of Murray's innovations was to place the Crazy Ads strategically toward the back of the bus. No longer did drivers have to plead with people to "step to the rear please." Passengers were delighted to read their way to the rear.

Then the ads started disappearing from the buses. Students were taking them down as souvenirs for bedroom walls. Some of the legitimate ones, too, that were a little wacky. However, Jay didn't let this bit of thievery bother him in the least, figuring it was good advertising that proved the high rack readership he claimed inside his buses.

Numerous phone calls came into the Twin Cities bus office from riders who wanted more information on the various jobs, services and items being advertised. And most all the callers were quite serious! There was more than a bit of interest in these particular ads:

ACT NOW!

Let us drill in your home. Our crew of 200 miners are waiting to drill until we find something. You may be living over valuable coal, oil or uranium! Pay nothing until we find something. If you've got it, we'll get it.

BUILD YOUR OWN HOME

Use unusual and enviable day-old bread blocks. Only six months of aging turns our bread into cement-like blocks. Your choice of whole wheat, rye or pumpernickel home. Send for low cost plans.

FOR RENT

$100 bill. Impress your neighbors. Use to establish credit. Attract new friends. Only 75 cents a day or $3.50 a week. Also have $50 bill available for lower rates.

When callers to Murray's office learned the ads were just gags, many reacted with disappointment or annoyance at having been taken. Some were relieved to learn what they suspected.

Within six months the advertising racks were completely sold out to legitimate sponsors and Jay had no more use for the Crazy Ad fillers. Just to prove their success story, he hired a research organization to take an independent poll. They made a comprehensive survey of bus riders, without using visual reminders, and discovered that 84.9 per cent of the respondents remembered and approved of the Crazy Ads.

Letters continued to arrive at the bus company offices

asking about some of the items advertised through the Crazy Ads. Things like rare hangnails, barnacle removers, instant air, portable holes, army cookbooks, pyramids, used cannon balls and a caboose. A favorite request was for the "hand grenades painted red and green. Ideal for Christmas presents."

Meantime, the Crazy Ad movement had begun to spread to transportation vehicles in other cities when radio and television personalities such as Johnny Carson, Arthur Godfrey, Dave Garroway and Henry Morgan read the ads to their audiences.

Godfrey read a number of the ads on his CBS radio show with Victor Borge as his guest who then asked, "Do they *really* put them on the buses?"

"Yes," replied Godfrey. "Very funny, too. Alan Abel tells me they got some replies. I learned long ago there are always people who will take you seriously. About twenty years ago I had a program in New York. And I was on for some cereal or other. I can't remember what it was, fortunately. When the sponsor left me I said, 'This program is brought to you by Clavintrude.' And that everybody ought to have some Clavintrude. And you could buy it by the quart in a hardware store. Don't you know, people went to the stores and asked for it? So I gave that up. No, you don't fool around with things they're serious about."

The *Saturday Review*'s Jerome Beatty, Jr., devoted a full column to the Crazy Ad campaign, saying in part * :

Straphangers in Minneapolis, St. Paul, Duluth and other cities in that part of the country have been reading the display-advertisements in buses with more than the usual avidity. It's not that they are particularly looking for what kind of toothpaste or savings bank to use, but that they are

* Copyright 1958 Saturday Review, Inc.

hoping to find another Crazy Ad. A Crazy Ad is just that—a screwy one that is sandwiched in among the legit ones, the idea being to make the riders read them all. Here's a sample:

WANTED

Clerk-cellist, with long hair. Must have own airplane and speak fluent Danish. Prefer art collector who is not afraid to go out and meet people. Old established shoe firm. Between fittings play a few hairy tunes.

Or you're apt to see a Crazy Ad which calls for a man with experience to sell "Stradivarius-like violins." The crazy fellow behind the ads is Alan Abel, whose only problems have been (1) thinking up new copy, (2) keeping up with orders, (3) replacing Crazy Ads that are stolen by admirers, and (4) answering letters from folks who take them seriously. Abel is busy trying to convince the right people to put Crazy Ads in the New York subways. He's already got the first one picked out:

MONEY! MONEY! MONEY!

We've got what you want. Borrow up to $82.50. Your word is as good as cash! No credit references, no security, not even your own signature required. We deduct each week from your salary until the sum you need has accumulated with our Mr. Briggs.

This *Saturday Review* piece encouraged Mark Elsis, advertising manager for the New York Subway System, to make a valiant but vain effort to sell his bosses on trying the Crazy Ads. However, they were afraid the subway riders wouldn't be able to distinguish the Crazy Ads from the real ones. When I suggested that the Transit Authority raise the fare from twenty to fifty cents, to attract a more literate class of passenger, they didn't appreciate my suggestion.

Various bus companies around the country began demanding more Crazy Ads than I could create so I employed the services of writer-actor-comedian George Wayne. Bernad Creations, the novelty company that had made a huge success with Herb Gardner's cartoon "Nebishes," licensed the use of Crazy Ads on numerous household and office items, including matchbook covers, ashtrays and wall plaques.

Teen Digest, a Parents Institute publication for the high school and college markets, purchased a flock of the Crazy Ads along with a contest that would allow their readers to create a few themselves. Winners were to receive ten dollars for each one published.

The contest produced thousands of entries. Some of the kids were especially clever. And several of the winning ads were strangely familiar to me. They turned out to be exact copies of ads that George and I had created for bus companies in Peoria, Illinois, and Sioux Falls, South Dakota! Thereafter, the editors of *Teen Digest* retained a copy of all our ads.

World Pacific Records, producers of the Carl Reiner-Mel Brooks album, "The 2000 Year Old Man," offered to make an album of Crazy Ads. So, with the help of George Carter, another comedy writer, and George Wayne, Jeanne and I worked around the clock to prepare a comedy script incorporating the ads. Two days later I flew up to Plattsburgh, New York, for a live performance at the State Teachers College and recorded "The Best of Crazy Ads" album. The students and faculty reacted in all the right places—and some unexpected ones—to such nonsense as:

Now here is an interesting ad I found on page three of the Plattsburgh Daily Disappointment: "For sale. Slightly used caboose. Just painted bright red. Sleeps two. Ready to roll. One-hundred feet of railroad track free! First $200 takes it. Come to B.&O. freight yard after midnight and ask for Joe. Bring a flashlight, tow truck, chain and the cash." Here's another ad. "Do you live alone? Are you unhappy? Is your mailbox empty? Your telephone silent? Then let us send you salesmen to brighten your day, bills to flood your mail, and friendly calls from our collection agency."

The Citadel Press published a collection of Crazy Ads to coincide with the album and a minor national craze seemed to be under way among people of all ages. There was something for everybody. Kids went for the ones that offered weird things like, "Girogges for sale. . . . At last our laboratory has crossed a lovable giraffe with the frisky frog to produce the wacky, tame and loyal Girogge. Only two to a customer." Adults preferred ones like: "Salesmen! Sell collapsible homes for big turnover profits. Sell home to family and then refund 50 per cent when it collapses six weeks later. Sell same home many times. Free life insurance, disguises and bail bond."

A few weeks after the Crazy Ad book was on the market its sales slumped to practically zero after a magnificent start. Jeanne and I went out to check a few of the larger bookstores in Manhattan when, lo and behold, we saw loads of Crazy Ad books in window displays and on counters. Only they were *counterfeit* copies!

They were printed offset—an exact duplicate of the original book. Only the counterfeiters left off the writer credit and the publisher credit and the copyright notice that supposedly protects the rights of an author. People outside the entertainment medium don't find such thievery much to gripe about. But it can be likened to the theft of a more tangible property. If someone stole your car, for instance, you'd be pretty sore about it. And while you may collect on your insurance, an author, unfortunately, has no such protection of his property.

Citadel Press executives were just as infuriated as I over this discovery but refused to act, claiming it was too costly to track down the counterfeiters and bring them to justice, and impossible to capture any of their profits. When I had queried bookstore clerks and managers about their source of supply for the counterfeit Crazy Ad books, they shrugged their shoulders innocently and remained mum. Finally, the Citadel Press halted their printing of the book because they couldn't compete with the counterfeit edition.

Since counterfeiting of published material is a federal offense, under the Copyright Law of 1909, punishable by a fine of a thousand dollars, a year in jail or both, I next went to the F.B.I. My complaint included the following documentary evidence: eleven by fourteen photographs of the window displays and store racks with Crazy Ad counterfeits, signed purchase receipts for the ones I bought as evidence and a complete history of the chain of events.

The F.B.I. agent who handled my case told me it was going to be a while before they could pursue it, mainly because they were quite busy at the time chasing jewel thieves, bank robbers and dope smugglers. I would just have to wait my turn. I said I understood and shook hands with him, proud to know that Uncle Sam's G-men would someday bring the culprits to justice.

While visiting an Upper East side bookstore dealing in paperbacks, I struck up a conversation with a wholesale jobber who claimed that the Crazy Ad books were probably handled by a distributor in California.

At last I had my first concrete lead on the source of

supply. And, fortunately, Jeanne and I were headed for California in about three weeks to lecture in schools and colleges.

We drove to California and made periodic stops in bookstores; counterfeit copies of my book were everywhere. In Los Angeles I checked with an assistant district attorney and he wasn't too encouraging. I learned I would have to present indisputable evidence on the existence of counterfeit printing plates before any kind of raid could take place.

In a run-down section of a sleepy little college town, Jeanne and I walked into a small combination greeting-card store and print shop that was part of a house. The proprietor was a slim man in his late forties. While Jeanne shopped around the display area for cards, I posed as a specialty salesman looking for a job in the Los Angeles area.

"Wish I could help you, fellow," he said, "but we're all set."

"I like your line of cards," I ventured as I strolled toward the back room. An offset printing machine had just started up, but he blocked my way.

"I'm sorry, you'll have to excuse me now," he said with finality.

That's the way we left things. And it was frustrating. There were Crazy Ad books on display in his front window and the ones on his counter seemed "factory fresh." He just had to be doing the printing, shipping and selling—profiting at my own and my legitimate publisher's expense. But under the law I didn't have any right to do anything about it. Reluctantly we left empty-handed, hoping that the F.B.I. would soon do the job.

NINE

THE BETTER BUSINESS BUREAU IS WATCHING YOU

After three months of touring schools and colleges in California, Jeanne and I returned to New York to find plenty of trouble waiting for me. I was being investigated by the National Better Business Bureau. They had been summoned by their Peoria, Illinois, chapter as a result of this Crazy Ad that had appeared on local buses:

BUSINESS OPPORTUNITY

Make money at home like we do. Raise and sell your own squid. Harmless and lovable. Wonderful as companion. Will eat anything. Especially fond of children. Small investment will bring you initial shipment of 200 squid. Watch them multiply! No phone orders or C.O.D.'s. Write: Crazy Ads, Transit Advertising.

I searched through my files and found only two letters forwarded to me by the transit advertising company that may have touched off the interest from the Better Business Bureau. One from a woman who lived in a town near Peoria read:

Dear Sir:

I am interested in knowing more about your squid. As a retired elementary school teacher I would like to start my own business. I love animals, fish and children and your squid offering sounds like the kind of light home activity I could handle.

Please advise full details such as space needed, how squid are cared for and whether you supply a training manual. Thank you.

Yours very truly,
A former teacher

Dear Teacher:

Thank you for your letter. I'd like to discourage you from raising squid. It's very dirty work, you're up half the night with them, and they are more incorrigible than unruly kids.

So please take my advice and find something else you might enjoy doing. Good luck!

Sincerely yours,
Alan Abel

The other letter was from a Peoria banker:

Dear Sirs:

I noticed your ad for squid on the bus this morning and I would appreciate knowing the following information:

1. The basic cost per squid.
2. Complete information on their upkeep.
3. Names of buyers in Peoria who can vouch for their safety with children.

4. Information on your company.

Thank you for your cooperation.

> Yours very truly,
> Banker

Dear Banker:

Thanks for your letter. Our squid are $2500 each, cash on the line. We'll send you a nice bunch of mixed males and females . . . absolutely no queers guaranteed . . . on a railroad flat car packed in dry ice, F.O.B. Takes about 48 hours to thaw them out. Then watch them live! Can't give out any information on satisfied customers as this is confidential; ditto for info on our company. You'll just have to take your chances with us.

> Regards,
> Alan "Buggsy" Abel

Now I can't imagine anyone in his right mind taking me seriously, especially a banker, but it's possible he ran all the way to his local Better Business Bureau. A letter from their national office in New York asked me to "kindly review the attached form and favor us with your reply immediately."

The form was a request for a complete financial statement on my company's activities with squid. I replied that I would not furnish such information because it might be considered an invasion of privacy.

"Furthermore, my dear sir," I added. "Such confidential statistics are made available only under the condition that you permit our accountants to go over *your* books. This seems fair, doesn't it?"

The Representative's next letter ignored my challenge and stated:

Dear Mr. Abel:

About a month ago we received advice from the Better Business Bureau in Peoria, Illinois, that advertising was appearing on car cards in that city offering "squid for sale, harmless and lovable, wonderful as companion, watch them multiply, etc." Was this advertising placed by your company? If so, details of the offer would be helpful to us so that we can reply to the Peoria Better Business Bureau.

Yours very truly,
Representative

This was becoming absurd. If the Peoria Better Business Bureau had contacted their local transit advertising agency, they would have been told the ads were gags. Or they might have taken a look at some of the other Crazy Ads running on their buses, such as:

WILL SACRIFICE:
Pyramids over 10,000 years old. Ideal for mooring Zeppelins, drying fish, or hanging a large laundry. Must be seen to be appreciated. Only 2 to a customer. No brokers or samples, please!

LET ME CHANGE YOUR FACE
Former plastic surgeon will make you look like your favorite movie or TV star. Mrs. Lela Jones of Boston said: "I was amazed when I looked in the mirror and saw Ronald Reagan." No money down. Easy life payments.

On the other hand, maybe it's just as well they didn't notice these ads. I might have been in more hot water!

It was now time to nip this squid business in the bud. I addressed my next communique directly to the President of the Better Business Bureau with a carbon copy to their Peoria branch.

President
National Better Business Bureau, Inc.
Chrysler Building
New York, New York
Dear Sir:

In response to your request for information on our squid I would like to state that we are offering squid for sale not only in Peoria, Illinois, but also St. Paul, Minneapolis, Philadelphia, San Antonio, St. Louis, Pittsburgh and other cities across the country! *Nor have we received a single complaint from any of these other cities or any requests for privileged information on our company.*

Now I'll tell you what I'm going to do, in order to resolve this situation between you and your Peoria bureau. I will send them a sample squid out of a shipment that has just arrived from Peru. His name is "Roger" and he is housebroken. I'm sure the people in your office out there will find many moments of pleasure playing with him during coffee breaks.

Please advise the Peoria Better Business Bureau to prepare for Roger's arrival; they will need a 30 x 60 foot tank with at least five feet of water, slightly salted. A complete training manual will be furnished that teaches Roger to sit up and beg, fetch things, roll over, answer the door and even growl at strangers such as process servers, policemen and Federal agents.

Finally, his favorite food is goldfish. He gets along nicely on five or six a day.

> Yours very truly,
> Alan Abel

After I had mailed the letter, I wondered if I hadn't made a mistake, the way things were going. I began to envision them out there in the Peoria office actually waiting for my "shipment." It would serve them right if I did send a sample. In any case, I thought I'd better take out some insurance. I called up the Fulton Fish Market.

"You want squid? Sure we got it."

"Now, those are *live* squid, aren't they?"

"Live squid! No. These aren't alive."

"But you advertise fresh fish . . ."

"Yeah. But 'fresh' ain't *live*."

"Fresh fish are fresh *dead*, huh?"

"Well, it takes maybe a couple days for the boats to get here, you know. But they're perfectly good."

"But the squid I need has to be alive. I might be in more trouble if I mail a dead one."

"Mail?"

I tried to explain as simply as possible why I needed a live squid and that I had to send it to Illinois. And it had to be a male because I'd already named him Roger. I was surprised the guy was still on the line.

"How can you tell the difference between a male and a female squid?" I asked. "Do you have a different number of tentacles or something?"

"You got me, fella. I just sell 'em. I don't get involved in their personal lives."

The president didn't answer my letter. Two days later I received a wire from Peoria that said simply: SEND NO SQUID. REPEAT. SEND NO SQUID. DO NOT SEND SQUID.

I was just as relieved, as I'm sure they were, that I didn't have to follow through on this particular hoax.

But there was another prospective problem maker, this time in St. Louis. And the Crazy Ad he responded to read:

FOR RENT

Bathroom. Private entrance. Fully equipped including telephone and hi-fi. Plenty of hot water. Prefer

non-smoking business man or quiet Ivy-League type.
Near bus stop. Write Box _____ 507 Fifth Avenue,
N.Y.C.

I received a special delivery letter from an **R. W.** who
wrote:

Gentlemen:
   I am desperately in need of a bathroom. The one you
advertised near the bus stop sounds O.K. I am enclosing
a $5 deposit. Please do not keep me waiting too long.
                                          Sincerely,
                                          R. W.

I returned his five dollars with a one sentence note:
"Sorry R. W., present tenant has decided to stay on."

It was nearly four years later when I received a call
from the F.B.I. with a report on my Crazy Ad book. But
all the agent could tell me was that by the time they investigated my case, too many years had gone by and the
counterfeiter's trail was dead. There was nothing more
they could do about it.

TEN

I WAS AN
AUSTRALIAN SPY

In the spring of 1966, Peter Verstappen, an account executive with Bruce Friedlich advertising, called me to ask if I had ever been a spy. I said I hadn't but always thought it would be fun to try sometime. Verstappen had the perfect opportunity and wanted me to work up a believable routine as an undercover agent. He was launching a campaign to introduce Foster's lager beer in America from Australia and his first project was to greet members of the beer industry at a special luncheon in two weeks. My job would be to address them as an Australian spy named Thompson Johnson Kettleby Rundle.

I assimilated everything I could about Australia. Jeanne coached me with a cockney accent, but I kept lapsing into an Irish brogue with traces of a Liberace-Ed Sullivan mixture. Dialects just aren't my bag! So we decided to forget the accent and pretend I was a spy who was so good I'd erased every trace of Aussie speech when I infiltrated the American culture.

On the appointed day at New York's Tavern-on-the-Green, I was introduced seriously from the dais. Stealthily I approached the microphone and spoke to the three hundred or so guests:

"Yes, my name is Thompson Johnson Kettleby Rundle. Fifteen years ago today I left Australia for America on a top secret mission. As a counteragent for United Breweries of Melbourne, my job was to study the drinking habits of people in this country by infiltrating cocktail parties, taverns and the 5:10 to Westport. I was to report back to Foster's from time to time so they could eventually corner the beer-drinking market away from all competitors.

"Now the code name for this confidential operation was 'Bottleneck.' As an Aussie spy in America I had to change my entire way of life. First and foremost, I had to learn to think like an American, act like one, dress like and speak like one. And I think I did it rather well. Because I can now pass for any American citizen. In fact, I'm so convincing, when I return to visit Australia, customs officials won't believe my legitimate passport!

"I've fooled more darn people. I even fooled some Arizona Indians once. They thought I was from New Zealand! While traveling about the States I used an ordinary American name, John Smith. The only time I had trouble with this identity was when registering at hotels —because I usually checked in alone.

"You're probably wondering if I was ever detected or

had narrow escapes. Well, there were two. One bloke
found me out because he was married to my sister's husband and could recognize me on sight. I offered him fifty
pounds—excuse me, fifty dollars—if he would jump like
a kangaroo down Fifth Avenue. He did it and the men in
the white suits took him away. That's the last I ever
heard from him. And I still have the fifty pounds! Dollars!!

"Another close shave was the time a salesman from a
big United States beer company tried to expose me.
Imagine, he thought there was something funny about the
way I walked! Fortunately, he exposed himself first. And
I merely had him arrested.

"You're probably wondering about my name, Thompson Johnson Kettleby Rundle. Where does it come from?
Well, let me explain. My mother was Katherine Kettleby
from Hokitika, New Zealand. She was a most unusual
fortune teller with *two* crystal balls. When my father,
John Rundle, dropped by to have his palm read, she accidentally broke one of her balls. It was a fateful accident
and they were married nine months later. My second
name—Johnson—was the name of a neighbor's yacht where
I was conceived. And the first name, quite frankly—
Thompson—was taken from the telephone directory. They
just threw a dart at the 'T' section.

"I was educated at the Geelong Grammar School at
Timbertop, the same one attended by Prince Charles.
And my father had no visual signs of income as long as
I can remember—because he was extremely wealthy.

"During the second World War I joined the Royal
Army Air Forces, where I received a commission as an
officer with the Australian security police—the ZED Force
which was connected with the M-15 Group in England.

My first mission was to disguise myself as a civilian and cruise among the islands in the South Pacific. Armed only with cans of Foster's beer, my task was to bring the Japanese out of the caves where they were hiding. I found that a can of Foster's at the end of a string was much better than a grenade. It really was. We not only had a live prisoner our side could interrogate, but we also had a potential Foster's beer drinker! Why else do you think we have such big Foster sales in Japan right now?

"I personally captured the great Japanese General Go-Go Pashamimi in a cave on Norwalk Island. He not only followed the can of beer on the string out of his cave, but he also surrendered the entire Japanese navy to me! And for only two cases of Foster's lager beer. I received the Order of the British Empire for this feat. Of course, the surrender paper was never honored by Tojo. He was sore as hell because Pashamimi sold out for only two cases. Actually, the General had no authority to surrender the navy because he was an army man. How stupid can you get? Also, he had used the wrong military surrender form—879-O.K., a requisition for bamboo fishing poles.

"Anyhow, General Pashamimi is alive and well today in Tokyo. He's made a fortune manufacturing breakable thread for men's suits being exported to America. We still exchange Christmas cards. No matter what your feelings might be about the Japanese and World War II, don't ever forget, they're still giving us the business.

"So I'm glad to welcome Foster's beer to America. Just let me read you a few testimonial letters from Australia:

Gentlemen:
    I thought you might like to know that I was declared

the winner in a beer drinking contest held last week in Sydney. I drank fifty-two bottles of Foster's lager beer in two hours.

Yours sincerely,
H. S.
c/o St. Vincent's Hospital

"And here's another one:

Dear Sirs:

At one time I was an unemployed girl who long suffered from a bashful personality. I was also a wall-flower. Then I started drinking Foster's lager beer and it made me confident. Thanks to you people, today I am a successful truck dispatcher in Brisbane.

Dimples

"I would like to show you several interesting charts. Now study the figures carefully, please. Notice that for every 200 tons of Foster's beer shipped to the States from Australia, only 182.9 tons arrive. We have discovered that greedy, thirsty crew members cannot wait to get their beer on arrival. They have been dipping into the ship's hold en route, breaking open cases and drinking. Naturally these costs were deducted from their final wages.

"According to statistics, 87 per cent of all shipwrecked sailors preferred to send their distress messages in a Foster's lager beer bottle! And 54 per cent of the messages arrived safely—as opposed to those sent in a Brand X bottle. Unfortunately, I have no statistics on the number of sailors actually rescued. But at least their messages did get through.

"Here is another interesting survey showing the relationship between Foster's beer drinkers and the number of kangaroos in Australia. Notice there are more beer drinkers than there are kangaroos. Armed with information like this, perhaps you can understand why Foster's has been obliged to engage me in cloak and dagger work."

After the lecture and luncheon I was besieged by several dozen people including a few reporters. I hadn't been exposed as a hoaxer and I realized by their questioning that these people believed me! One fellow from Australia actually thought I was on Norwalk Island during the war and mentioned that he used to fly over it regularly. Another man asked me questions about "Chloe," a famous nude painting over a bar in Melbourne, since he hadn't been back in some ten years. I said it was still there, but full of dart holes. Did they really buy my story—that I'd lost an Australian accent? That I was a spy? After all the laughs?

The next day, when reporter Walter Carlson wrote a straight story on the event in *The New York Times*, I assumed that he too must have taken me seriously.

By keeping a straight face and pretending sincerity—in spite of all the obvious jokes—I had been able to bamboozle the audience. The advertising agency was pleased with my performance, as were the Foster's executives present, and I felt good about this. That is until I learned accidentally that a live kangaroo mascot at the party received the same fee I did. And the kangaroo did nothing but mess on the floor!

ELEVEN

THE NEWSPAPER
THAT NEVER WAS

In 1963, I attempted to sell to newspaper syndicates a humor column I had created entitled "The Private World of Prof. Bunker C. Hill." The professor offered such solid ideas as "How to Live on $3 a Week," "How to Scratch an Itch in Public" and "How to Neutralize a Nasty Neighbor," among others. After about twenty rejections from the major distributors of feature material to newspapers, I figured they weren't interested.

Next I tried selling the column to newspapers direct, by mailing a press release and samples to one hundred of the largest daily newspapers. There were about seven replies, all negative.

I suppose I should have given up at this point. But I recalled my college days when I had written a strong letter of condemnation to the publisher of *Down Beat* music magazine, complaining about his weak column features. In the return mail I received a challenge from the editor to put some words where my mouth was. So I did. And my colmun ran in *Down Beat* until I graduated.

But if I were to get a hearing for my satirical columns from the key newspaper executives, I'd have to find an unorthodox way to get their attention. Thus far, all my submissions had been rejected by the assistants to the assistants who screen new material. If every important newspaper had dismissed Prof. Hill, what other way was there to get him published outside of starting a newspaper myself? That was it! That was the idea I'd been looking for.

I would publish my own newspaper. Or at least create such an illusion. But where? In what city? That was an easy decision. The San Francisco *Chronicle* had a style that was flamboyant, imaginative and entertaining. Although they had rejected my column initially, I wasn't discouraged. I made up a press release that announced a new California newspaper to be called *The San Francisco Times*:

FOR IMMEDIATE RELEASE

Announcement has been made by a private investor from New York that San Francisco will soon have a fourth newspaper, *The San Francisco Times*. Full coverage of world, national, state and city news is to be handled in an unusual manner that will permit the use of a "hard cover book" technique. Each issue will integrate all the news into a single episodic story.

For instance, Page One will begin: "The weather in the Bay Area was predicted to be fair with little change. In Washington the President called a cabinet meeting to discuss the latest Soviet threats to world peace; and while they were meeting three liquor stores in San Mateo were robbed at gunpoint. Further details will be reported later on in this story concerning last night's vice raid on Market Street. Meantime, the stock market reported a normal amount of activity and Johnny Carson announced that Governor Reagan and his wife Nancy would appear on his show *Tonight* in a skit written by former White House press secretary Pierre Salinger entitled "Show Me the Way to Go Home."

Full details on *The San Francisco Times'* editorial staff will be announced shortly.

This press release was mailed to newspapers, radio and television stations in California. Within forty-eight hours I had received calls from the West Coast. Reporters for stations and newspapers wanted further details; however, I explained that I was under a news blackout from my boss and they would have to wait until my arrival shortly in San Francisco.

Jeanne was all for the idea of our visiting San Francisco. The trip would only be exploratory because there was no promise that the results would justify the expenditure. But on the basis of the initial response to my first press release, I felt confident my "newspaper" would produce results—although I wasn't sure how or when. Besides, we began to long for a lobster dinner at the Wharf and a forty-nine-way sundae at the Nut Tree in nearby Vacaville. Also, our former apartment was available.

I mailed out another press release from New York the day before we flew to San Francisco:

FOR IMMEDIATE RELEASE

Temporary assignments for staff positions with *The San Francisco Times* have been announced by publisher J. Donald Barker from his Upstate New York headquarters. They are as follows:

T. Frederick Thornton ....Managing Editor
Angela Bidwell Cassingham ....Society Editor
Hopwood Ferrie ....Editorials
Mary Margaret Pointer ....Farm News
Cynthia Lansing York III ....Personal Advice
Abdul Zanzibar ....Foreign News
Beaureguard "Hoot" Gibson ....Film Reviews

For further details contact Bruce Spencer, 2434 Vallejo Street in San Francisco. Telephone: WAlnut 6-0056.

No sooner had we opened the door to our apartment than the phone began to jangle. The first call was from a man who identified himself as attorney Jake Erlich, who had heard about *The San Francisco Times* and claimed he owned the title. I challenged him on whether anybody could lay claim to words in the public domain, especially since he hadn't actually started publication of a newspaper with such a name. "Mr. Erlich" hung up abruptly and I then wondered if it really could have been the famed attorney.

Next came a call from television station KPIX with a request for an interview on the six o'clock news that evening. I promised to be there, hoping I wouldn't run into the station manager, Ray Hubbard. He was one of the unsuspecting Westinghouse executives I had been hired to tease at a broadcasting convention and I could hardly expect him to welcome me with open arms.

Don Sherwood, a personality with KGO-TV, requested an appearance. Tom Eastham, managing editor of the *News—Call—Bulletin,* called and wanted all the information he could get. So did reporters from the *Examiner* and the *Chronicle.* I gave them only vague details, claiming they would have to wait for a general press conference in a few days.

I then dashed over to the KPIX television studios and was just in time for the news that was being presented live. Somebody motioned me into a chair, threw a mike around my neck and we were on the air:

"A news announcement has been made from New York that San Francisco will soon have a fourth newspaper, *The San Francisco Times,*" said the announcer. "The public relations director for the publisher is Bruce Spencer who is here with us now. Mr. Spencer, what type of paper will the *Times* be?"

"Well, it's going to be opposed to the normal run of newspapers. That is, we plan not to be a victim of the news pressures and the penalties of deadlines. We want to write the news leisurely and in a very truthful kind of way. We'll cover everything that's happening with lots of research and color without regard to a deadline. It's going to be tabloid size, coming out late in the afternoon, hopefully. The premise of the paper will be based upon more latitude in saying what we want to say without becoming bogged down by the mechanics of fighting the clock. Another thing, our paper will *not* take sides if we don't believe in either one; we will show as wide an attitude as possible, letting the public decide what is best for them. This will be a people's paper, a paper of the people. For example, when a new show opens at the Opera House we'll have a review by a housewife in San Rafael. We'll let someone who washes clothes, handles kids and knows about life as it really is do our reviewing. This way people can feel it's their newspaper as well as ours. . . ."

News reporter Don Bryce asked me why investors would put a fourth newspaper in San Francisco when they were already having difficulty supporting three in that market.

"This is one market we've studied very carefully, Mr. Bryce, and found that it is ripe for something new and different. And we intend to rise above journalistic mediocrity that has permitted only a few papers to survive. Now I know this is high and mighty and a lot of people are going to say 'prove it.' Nevertheless, I believe we're sitting on a lot of optimism."

Bryce asked me if I was the same person connected with the Society for Indecency to Naked Animals.

"Yes, I handled the public relations for that very eccentric organization. Fortunately, I resigned from them in order to devote full time to the newspaper now. As a matter of fact, Mr. Bryce, I'm glad you brought up my past track record because we did such a bang-up job in promoting that organization throughout the world."

Bryce asked me point blank if the *San Francisco Times* was a practical joke.

"Why a joke?" I replied vehemently. "Would I be sitting here if I were a joke? Would this station be on the air if it were a joke? Would you be asking me such a question if it were a joke? I don't know. Because you never know how serious a person really is when he's promoting something and perhaps putting many hours in it. . . ."

Bryce next suggested that there was something strange about the absence of my publisher's name with either Dun & Bradstreet or the Newspaper Guild.

"I dare say, Mr. Bryce, that any cursory examination you may have made about the authenticity of *The Times,* or its people, is based only upon the lack of authoritative information at your disposal, which of course does not allow you to make an accurate judgment . . . people may wonder why our publisher isn't out here in front to meet the press personally. Well, why haven't people been able to interview Howard Hughes, or Greta Garbo, or Freddie Bartholomew? You know, people searched for years to find out the name of Mark Twain and they were embarrassed to learn it was really Samuel L. Clemens. Why did Bernie Schwartz change his name to Tony Curtis? Was World War II a promotion gimmick for uniform manufacturers? I doubt it. You see, it's possible to draw all kinds of erroneous conclusions by putting together unrelated facts that seem related. I don't know whether this makes sense to you or not, but I find it difficult to explain my position in the light of the assorted pieces of evidence that suggest anything else to the contrary. For example, the only defense against libel and slander is the truth. Now our newspaper is going to swear by this theory. Another thing, our comics are going to be funny. No moral messages. I may be straying a bit from time to time here but I want to emphasize how vital and challenging *The San Francisco Times* will be. . . ."

Don Bryce and his news staff that included reporters Nancy Clark and Glen Hanson seemed to have had enough of me. I was coldly dismissed by Bryce with his closing comments: "Thank you very much. We've had as our guest on the Big News tonight Bruce Spencer, associated with the coming publication of a fourth newspaper in San Francisco to be known as *The San Francisco Times*."

I left the studio uncertain whether my "circumlocution" on the air was believable enough to keep the new newspaper image alive; I was surprised Bryce didn't dismiss me abruptly because of my past association with

S.I.N.A.—especially since he correctly read the hoax angle —or at least pursue this lead more relentlessly.

When I reached our apartment Jeanne was on the phone taking messages down as fast as she could answer and write. At that point, I must confess, I realized I had a tiger by the tail. But my motive was quite simple: I wanted to create enough word-of-mouth talk about this new paper in San Francisco so I could meet the top executives of the *Chronicle* on a more or less equal footing. Then I hoped to be able to sell them my column.

If I were to strike out on selling Prof. Bunker C. Hill as a regular feature, I would at least have had the satisfaction of knowing that decision-making executives turned me down—not lower-echelon assistants to the editor.

Ira Blue, a late night interviewer from KGO radio, was one of the callers who saw me on KPIX's Big News and invited me on the air that night from 11 P.M. until 2 A.M. Jeanne was beginning to register concern that I might begin to take the situation so seriously I would go ahead and publish an issue. I had already thought of that, too. Especially since the idea was engendering such interest; perhaps a fourth newspaper was a very real possibility.

But I didn't want actually to produce a newspaper— even one issue that would contain a heavy sampling of my columns. I could never afford it, there were too many inherent problems with unions and I was going for the illusion, not the real thing.

Ira Blue's radio show was more of the same questions and answers. Only this time people called in on the air to discuss *The San Francisco Times* with me. I improvised some pretty wild ideas for this revolutionary paper about to make its debut; the image I drew seemed too fantasy-like for my own good, I thought. But during the taped commercials, Mr. Blue spoke to me quite seriously about the *Times*'s revolutionary philosophy.

The KGO radio publicity brought more phone calls at home the next day. One woman wanted to read me her poetry over the telephone; another man sang with a uke-lele to demonstrate his music ability to qualify as a critic; and an old-timer who claimed to have the largest collec-tion of mounted butterflies in the world offered to write a daily column on insects.

Suddenly I was turning on the whole nutty world! What kind of newspaper would *The San Francisco Times,* or any newspaper, be if it were really to be controlled by "the people"?

Someone called claiming he was a member of a news-paper union and wanted to know how many people would be employed by *The Times*. He sounded like a strong-arm type, with the typical tough voice and bad English.

"Well, when can I get a finger on the number of guys youse expect to handle?" he asked in a tone that demanded a prompt answer or else.

"I can't tell you that, sir. Mr. Barker, our publisher, is hunting wild boar in New Guinea for two months and the last time out he lost his larynx in a scrape with a native; so nobody can talk to him for at least a year."

"He's got to organize with the union. Otherwise there won't be no paper."

"He has considered the publication of *The Times* off-shore, on board a ship beyond the three-mile limit, in international waters, out of union reach."

"Come on, buddy. He'd never get his papers ashore without union boys."

"Haven't you ever heard of the tides? He could float in late afternoon editions on rubber rafts, just in time for the rush-hour traffic going home."

"Is he some kind of a rich nut or something?"

"I suppose you could say that."

"Well listen, fellow, we're ready to cooperate. We already got enough trouble with another strike maybe. So we don't need more trouble. Know what I mean?"

"All J. Donald Barker would have to hear is the threat of a strike and he'd pull his paper out of this market faster than you can blow your nose!"

"I'll do what I can to help, buddy. Just let me know."

He left his phone number and I put it in a handy place. There was never any telling when I might need a little muscle. But a pending strike? That was news to me.

As things turned out there wasn't a strike, although it came close. I was to learn only later that the impending *San Francisco Times* figured highly in the aversion of a general newspaper strike. The mediators reckoned with the loss of potential jobs if the new *Times* were to be scared away by a strike at that time. It was just a crazy coincidence; one that also gave a last-minute reprieve to the floundering *News-Call-Bulletin*.

Then came the news I had been waiting for—an invitation to have lunch with Scott Newhall, executive editor of the San Francisco *Chronicle*. His secretary, Miss Rhee, set a date for the following Friday.

I met Scott Newhall and Phelps Dewey, promotion manager for the *Chronicle,* in the dining room of the Clift Hotel, where we had a pleasant conversation about everything in the world except *The San Francisco Times*. Scott Newhall talked about my former crusade to clothe naked animals and commented on the cruel sense of humor that prompted so many people to think I wasn't serious. I agreed with him that it took a lot of gall for anyone to doubt the sincerity of my doings. Newhall spoke highly of my work in bringing to the world a sense of proportion and levity, at a time when moral decadence and hedonism were on the upswing.

Phelps Dewey didn't say much. He just listened. During dessert I felt it was time for my grandstand play.

"Gentlemen. I've enjoyed this luncheon, but I know you are both much too busy to spend so much time just eating. Undoubtedly you are on a fishing expedition to learn what you can about *The San Francisco Times*. Well, I was on the phone this morning with our publisher, J. Donald Barker. He admitted to me that he was in terrible financial straits, that he was depending on *me* to finance this paper. All along I thought *he* had the money!"

Phelps Dewey choked momentarily but soon regained his composure. Scott Newhall never flinched; he just cleared his throat and nodded for me to continue.

"So *The San Francisco Times* is now bankrupt. I trust you will retain this news in the greatest confidence. Now I have some rather bright information to go along with the bad. In my enthusiasm to assist this newspaper I went ahead and signed up a new columnist, Prof. Bunker C. Hill, for three years. I'm stuck with him. So I wonder if the *Chronicle* would consider buying out his contract from the defunct *San Francisco Times*?"

"I would be interested in examining the good Professor's work," Newhall said matter-of-factly. "And if he were to meet the standards of the *Chronicle,* there is always the possibility of adding him to our roster of columnists."

"Fine," I said. "I just happen to have a few samples of his work here with me."

Both Newhall and Dewey avoided looking at each other or me, otherwise I'm certain we would all have broken up. I handed over six sample columns and we went our separate ways.

A few days later I received a call from Miss Rhee. She asked if I could meet with Mr. Newhall that afternoon at 4 P.M. Naturally I said I would be there.

At the appointed time I met with Scott Newhall and Phelps Dewey in Mr. Newhall's office. They were both enthusiastic about Prof. Bunker C. Hill and had decided he would receive a six months' test run in the San Francisco *Chronicle*.

I wrote "The Private World of Prof. Bunker C. Hill" column from New York and it ran for two years in the *Chronicle*. The Professor commented on such subjects as "How to Avoid Tipping" and "Do-It-Yourself Home Analysis." I interviewed a cannibal and Adolph Hitler. And I solved problems: As a solution to our diminishing forests, I insisted that furniture manufacturers build chairs with only three legs instead of four. Because labor keeps asking for a four-day work week, I proposed to eliminate Wednesday from the calendar. "What do any of us do on a Wednesday that we couldn't do on a Tuesday or Thursday night instead?" I asked readers. And I proclaimed the abolishment of all schools "because kids don't like to go to school—they learn more from television—and, besides, can you recite even one thing you learned in the fifth grade?"

TWELVE

THE FALLACY OF
CREATIVE
THINKING

In October of 1965, Bob Novak, program manager of KDKA-TV in Pittsburgh, called me. His station was to play host in New York to the Associated Merchandising Corporation, an organization of advertising executives representing the largest department stores from all over the country. Novak wanted to entertain them with something more memorable than the usual pat-on-the-back speech that characterizes these conventions.

So it was Novak's idea to give them the unexpected, to hire me to pose as an expert in their own field, as an advertising and merchandising consultant. My job was to tell these executives how to run their business.

As I had once served time in an advertising agency, the chance to spoof a business that its practitioners take much

too seriously was a challenge I welcomed. And to be paid
to make satirical comment was an opportunity I couldn't
refuse.

Early one morning in January, 1966, the audience of
advertising heads had all assembled at Westinghouse's
Little Theatre just off Broadway where the *Merv Griffin
Show* is taped nightly. Seated in the chairs on the Griffin
set were a panel of prominent advertising men: Larry
Anderson, vice-president of Latent Image, Inc., a film production company; Tony Faillace, an independent commercial producer; and Marvin Davis, senior vice-president
of Delehanty, Kurnit & Geller advertising.

Unaware of my role, they each took their places before
the lectern and delivered sincere speeches on the theme
of the program, The Creative Process. And then samples
of their work were shown on film to the audience. I was
introduced by KDKA-TV station manager Paul O'Friel
who, besides Novak, shared in the secret:

"We're particularly pleased to welcome now a man who
has generated considerable comment in advertising circles. His unorthodox views have admittedly raised many
an eyebrow. Nevertheless, any objective attempt to ex-
plore the whole spectrum of creativity must provide a
platform for all points of view. Would you welcome please
the provocative spokesman and author of the highly controversial textbook, *The Fallacy of Creative Thinking.*
From the University of Ohio, Dr. Bruce Spencer."

I entered from behind the set, squinted at the bright
television lights, walked to the wrong side of the stage
and stumbled over a microphone cable along the way.
This entrance, I calculated, would disarm any of those
suspicious of my appearance on the program as an expert,

when no one had ever heard of me before. I wanted to epitomize those many puffy people of position who make great demands on others but who, if put on the spot to perform themselves, reveal a gross ineptitude.

"Ladies and gentlemen," I began grimly. "I have a prepared text for this address, but I'm not going to use it. I've been listening to these other speakers talk about creativity and, frankly, I'm a little annoyed. In fact, I'm *very* annoyed. Therefore, I'm going to throw my text away and speak only from my notes.

"I have a book—which has been out for a year now—entitled *The Fallacy of Creative Thinking*. It's a *text*—widely used by the Big Ten schools, the Big Seven, the Big Five. They all require this for students in marketing, advertising, public relations and journalism. I mention it because it attacks the problem of creativity right at the heart, and I'm not going to pull any punches here today either."

I felt the air of tension spread over my audience and the other three speakers now sitting to my right on stage. They hadn't expected such fire and brimstone tactics so early in the morning!

"These other speakers and I have a basic conflict of ideas. I respect their right to say what they say, but I can't go along with them. Now a lot of you are probably thinking, 'You're just a university man. What do you know about what's going on in the trade these days?' Well, let me point out that a week doesn't go by that I don't have at least one telephone call from the chairman of the board of a major department store chain. He calls me with his problems.

"Creative thinking is hogwash. That may be a shocking

statement, but it's true. I teach *formula* thinking, a concept based on the three S's—simplicity, sensationalism and
sales. At the end of the year, you don't call in your advertising people and ask them how stimulating their year
has been; you look at the balance sheets. The ledgers tell
you how successful your advertising has been. Theoreti-
cally it's great to sit around and talk about brainstorming
or creativity or commercial climate or point-of-purchase
displays, but what does it all mean on the profit and loss
columns?"

Now I had them going and everybody was getting a
little hot under the collar. This was the time to throw in
a few satirical haymakers, when they were least expecting
them.

"Ideas in this business are cheap. Good ideas, that is.
It's the *expensive* ideas that cost money. There's no such
thing anyway as a new idea, so why pay for them? The
best ideas are begged, borrowed or stolen. Take the slogan
'We Try Harder.' It was first used by a Virginia manufacturer during the Civil War that sold cannonballs to
the Confederates. They lost the war with that slogan.
Another slogan you think is new: 'It's What's Up Front
That Counts.' No. This was first used back in 1869 by a
firm that made brassieres.

"To excel is not to sell. That's why I teach my students
at the University of Ohio hard-core mediocrity. I tell
them that the key to successful selling in advertising today
is *deception.* And my advice to college graduates is: 'Don't
get caught.' I warn all my coeds that if they want to get
ahead in television they had better memorize and practice
the meaning of the FCC: Figure, Compromise, Consent.

"Listen to this letter from a former student of mine, a

young lady, twenty-two, brains, beauty—an I.Q. of 140—all the imagination in the world. She came to New York to work: 'Well, here I am, Dr. Spencer, slaving away at the ad agency for a big fat sixty dollars a week. Thanks to your teachings I have no illusions about this business. So I'm quitting next week to join the Peace Corps. Professor, remember that night last summer when we——' Well, that's personal.

"Take Chapter 11 in my book here, *The Fallacy of Creative Thinking,* entitled 'Damaged Goods, Marking Up and Miscellaneous Mischief.' I'll tell about the time last year when Macy's got stuck with fifty thousand pairs of Japanese binoculars. They couldn't give them away for love or money. I was called in secretly and I said to the boss, Mr. Yunich, 'This is a job for Jock the Jumper.' Now Jock is a professional suicide who will hang from the side of a building and threaten to jump. I used him once in San Francisco just before The White House went out of business. Well, we hired Jock to dangle from the fourth floor of Macy's for two hours and he attracted twelve thousand people in less than forty-eight minutes. Everybody likes to watch a suicide. One hundred hot-shot salesmen went through the crowd like greased lightning and in two hours had sold over twenty-two thousand pairs of Japanese binoculars! And at eight dollars a crack, marked up six dollars from wholesale. Now this is what I call practical selling. It's all in my book right here.

"Chapter 9 of my book describes the sales increase registered at a J. C. Penney store in Minneapolis when one 2 by 4 ad—just one small ad—was run announcing that at the end of thirty days, all prices would go up. Well, nothing went up—*except sales.* The people panicked, that's all.

We plotted it, researched it and sold it. Just look at this chart showing their dramatic sales rise during those thirty days. By the way this confidential chart was prepared by O'Rourke, Goldberg and Santini, . . . an integrated ethnic research firm that doesn't offend anybody.

"Then there was the thousand-dollar-bill promotion I devised for Goldblatt's in Chicago. A simple ad again: 'Any item over $5 purchased may contain a hidden thousand-dollar-bill.' Sales shot up. I knew they would, that's what I'm paid for. Sure I moonlight a bit; who can afford to live on the kind of money they pay university people nowadays? Anyhow, customers swarmed into the store and began buying everything in sight. We even had Mayor Daley on hand as a special added attraction and to keep things orderly. Now there *was* a thousand-dollar bill; we didn't want to get into trouble with the Better Business Bureau. But what shopper would think of looking in a brassiere, size 48-D? You don't have that kind of customer anymore!"

The audience was laughing in all the right places, but I suspected they just considered me a wacky professor.

"Another successful gimmick I've used is the Flickering Lights Sale. Don't laugh. Remember, it was Bill Bernbach who said recently in *The Wall Street Journal*, '85% of all advertising goes unnoticed, and you'd better be in that other 15%.' The Flickering Lights technique is simple. You just put a man in the basement at the master control switch and he switches the lights on and off all day long at two second intervals. This makes customers nervous. They figure something terrible is about to happen, so they buy nervously. Nothing happens except to your sales. And they just go up.

"In Chapter 14 of my book, entitled 'Never Trust a Resume,' I have outlined my own confidential lie-detector type of test for all new employees. Filene's department store in Boston adopted it only yesterday. Consider how you might answer these questions if you were a new employee:

1. Have you ever registered in a hotel or motel under an assumed name? Why?
2. Is anyone helping you with your answers? Who?
3. Did you tell a lie recently? When?
4. Are your palms perspiring? Why?
5. As a clerk in our store would you feel guilty about overcharging a wealthy customer? What portion of his purchase would you keep? How much would you give your mother?
6. On your previous job, were you ever caught with your hand in the till? About to go into the till? Having just left the till?
7. If your boss called you a thief would you hit him? Where?
8. Would you consider marrying the boss's daughter for money? For spite? Other?
9. Did you ever hide any earnings from your federal income tax? How much?
10. Would you care to reconsider your last answer?
11. Do you feel uneasy about answering any more questions?
12. Have you done any cheating on this test? (Use back side of questionnaire if necessary.)
13. Did you ever suggest an aspirin or a particular pill to anyone suffering from a headache or a cold?
14. How do you feel about people who practice medicine without a license?
15. Have you ever been arrested?
16. Would you call yourself a big liar, a medium one or a little one? Are you willing to swear to this?

"Now some of these questions are a little tricky, perhaps even sneaky. But the answers tell us who you are, what you are and why.

"I would like to see more department stores take advantage of what's happening in the headlines for special sales. People are tired of the Lincoln, Washington and Fourth of July sales. So why not do what Filene's did. On the day the Boston Strangler was convicted, they held a sale on women's silk stockings. At my suggestion, Halle Brothers in Cleveland had a customer stampede when they marked down their medicines and drugs the day Dr. Sam Sheppard was released from jail. And during the student riots in Berkeley, Rexall Drugs did their biggest business with a Looter's Day Special Sale.

"By the way, ladies and gentlemen, feel free to use any of these ideas I'm giving you because that's why I'm here. Perhaps you're wondering where I learned my basics in merchandising. Well, my dad taught me everything. He had a general store in Coshocton, Ohio, and during those thirty-five years in business he had 118 fire sales; he went out of business 206 times; and he kept a Distressed Merchandise Sale sign in the window constantly.

"I don't think anybody should ever forget the immortal words of Joseph L. Hudson, President of J.L. Hudson's department store in Detroit. He said, 'Competition today is something that enters the revolving door behind you and comes out in front of you.' Now stop and think about *that*.

"In closing, I'd like to return to my basic thesis: that creativity is impossible to create, and that only *formula* thinking can provide the solution to your marketing problems. At this time I'd like to inquire if anyone in the audience has a question about my work in the field of advertising and merchandising. No questions at all?"

"It's all very clear," sounded a cautious voice from the rear. There was subdued laughter at this comment and now I was certain my audience had been fooled.

"Let me say a final word," I continued.

"Just a moment, please, Dr. Spencer," interrupted Paul O'Friel. "I think it only fair at this time to advise the audience that you are a fraud!"

I shrugged my shoulders and sat down alongside the other panelists. A hushed silence remained over the auditorium. O'Friel continued:

"As we indicated earlier, creativity takes many sizes, shapes and forms. Putting this man on our panel was part of our *own* creativity. Let me just say that although he has written books, he never wrote the one I referred to earlier, that he is not Dr. Bruce Spencer at all, although he is from Ohio. So now, if I may reintroduce him—accurately—I'd like you to meet Alan Abel."

I acknowledged the courteous but restrained applause and headed for the stage door. En route, I passed panelist Tony Faillace who showed me his legal pad completely covered with challenges to just about every statement I had made. He was still flabbergasted.

A week later I received this letter from the advertising manager for Lazarus Department Store in Columbus, Ohio:

Dear Mr. Abel:

On behalf of the Advertising Managers of the Associated Merchandising Corporation, I want to express to you our deepest appreciation for the very creative program that you put on with the people from KDKA-TV.

As we returned to our meeting place, most of the group were still not over the shock of finding out that they were being spoofed. It was a hilarious presentation and I must say that you are a convincing actor. I want to thank you for making our meeting a very memorable one.

Sincerely,
Leonard R. Daloia

The success of the New York program prompted KDKA-TV to present it again, only this time in Pittsburgh for the benefit of their local radio, television and advertising people. My role was to be kept secret from everybody except the same three panelists, who, of course, now knew what to expect from me.

On the appointed afternoon we all did our "thing" in the Pittsburgh Playhouse before an audience of five hundred people in the trade. I played the bumbling professor and added a few new twists. For an opener I tried several jokes:

"I'm sure you are all familiar with rating services. One of them called a man at home one night and asked him 'Who are you listening to right now?' He answered, 'My wife.' "

That limp gag earned a slight chuckle. I gave them one more.

"Then there was this chap who didn't have a TV set. So he drilled a hole through his neighbor's apartment and watched wrestling every night—until he found out they didn't have a television set either."

This time there was a larger laugh, but I felt the strains of sympathy rippling through the audience. My mock fury took over and I presented an advertising spoof similar to the one in New York with a few alterations such as these:

"The best advertising plans are always thrown away. Let me tell you about Wastebasket Millie, a millionaire by day. But at night she works as a cleaning woman from midnight to dawn for the major ad agencies. She takes the ideas that are discarded in J. Walter Thompson wastebaskets and sells them to Young & Rubicam for fantastic money. Millie can spot a hot storyboard at thirty feet and stow it under her dress in five seconds flat. So if you want a good idea, look in your wastebaskets.

"Chapter 4 in my book is called 'How to Speak the Truth and Make It Sound Convincing.' Here I recommend the use of many charts and graphs such as these: *Always make sure your curves go up.* And as a clincher to making a successful pitch for a new campaign, wager a year's salary if the idea turns out to be a bomb. I don't know of any client who would hold you to your bargain.

"I was recently called in as a consultant . . . now please don't let this story get outside these walls—it's that confidential. A.T.&T. had a man they wanted to get rid of who was making sixty thousand dollars a year. My job was to persuade the man graciously to resign—because the company wanted to retain its reputation for never having fired anybody. But he was determined not to leave. Well, first I had his furniture removed from the office piece by piece. Now our purpose here was to give him a subtle hint that he wasn't wanted anymore. He stayed on. Then we turned up the temperature to eighty degrees so no matter what he did to the thermostat it wouldn't go down. He continued to work on the floor in his undershorts. Pretty tough guy. Next we established a Chinese water drip over his head from the floor above—one drop a second. This bothered him at first, but he got used to it. Finally we turned our big guns on him. Fire drills were held fourteen times a day during which he was the only participant. That did it. He resigned the next day. I know this may sound cruel to you people, but business is business."

During the final question and answer period an advertising man from the audience stood up and challenged me in an angry voice:

"We here in Pittsburgh have gotten along perfectly well without far-out campaigns and ideas such as you have stated and I would like to know about one example you can give, fully documented, of any of your successes by a radio station, television station or department store, with facts and figures, names of principal people involved. . . ."

On and on he droned, going from the initial question to an indictment of me and my methods, back to the question again and then on for more dialogue that vouched for the ways and means his people worked creatively. He was on the floor for at least five minutes before his final challenge:

"And what do you have to say to *that*, Dr. Bruce Spencer?"

From the scattered applause I gathered that the audience shared his contempt for me. I took a deep breath and replied casually into the microphone: "I'm sorry sir, I wasn't listening."

The theater rocked with laughter and Bob Novak took the opportunity to expose me as a hoaxer. Afterwards there was a cocktail party and as I mixed with the crowd I could feel again the overtones of shocked confusion at having been taken in by my spoof. My lecture contained just enough believability to make it seem real, enough zaniness to make it humorous.

I soon began to average a lecture a month as "Dr. Bruce Spencer—controversial consultant" and I experimented with even wilder ideas to toss at my audiences. They continued to listen to me seriously, took notes and asked probing questions afterwards. Once, before a group of San Francisco advertising men, I claimed to have started a new medium of advertising:

"We all know about Lady Bird Johnson's beauty campaign for removing the billboards from highways. This means media has to find new outlets to replace those billboards. I was asked by the Association of American Advertising Agencies to solve the problem. In two days I had the answer: Tap a source that has never been used before. But where? Well, I sweated it out in a steam bath at the New York Athletic Club and I saw the answer all around me among a dozen men. Why not rent the space on the 21 million bald-headed men in this country and use them as miniature mobile billboards? It's a natural for clients with small trade names like Coke, Hertz or Piels. For longer names we would use a string quartet with four bald musicians placed on stage so their message might read: 'Use Ban for B.O.' Of course their proper order would be imperative!"

I claimed to have two thousand bald-headed men standing by in New York ready to carry any message for two dollars a day per man. My charts and graphs showing the results of test market surveys with Bald-Headed Advertising—using bald-headed *Women* sitting in bus stops for passing auto traffic, and outside air terminals for low-

Gene Krupa manages a smile after being kidnaped by Ohio State students.

On the Mike Douglas Show, I implore Jayne Mansfield and Gypsy Rose Lee to cover their nude pets for the sake of decency.

The First Topless St
Quartet plays cham
music.

As moral crusaders, I
Henry and I inspect a b
dancer in San Francisco

As Julius Bristol, "Golf Pro," I taught broadcasting executives how to improve their game at the NAB Convention in Chicago.

The Ed Sullivan Show

"There's nothing wrong with me. . . . I live on the same floor in an apartment building with a psychiatrist and I give him a trumpet lesson every week in exchange for an hour on his couch. He's pronounced me perfectly sane!"

An outraged taxpayer challeng[es] Yetta's campaig[n] manager while su[p]porters Mimi Mill[er,] Jeanne Abel a[nd] doorman Bill Mor[e] look on.

Mrs. Yetta Bronstein, followed by her campaign manager, is photographed by Sam Falk for The New York Times.

Mrs. Yetta B[ron]stein's campaig[n for] Mayor of New [York] City.

To Yetta Bronstein, with best wishes from Richard Nixon.
(Copyright by Philippe Halsman)

Posing as a "professional consultant" before a convention of department-store advertising executives.

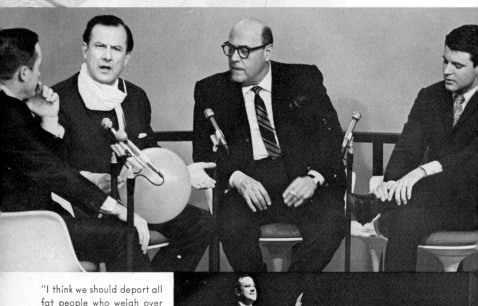

"I think we should deport all fat people who weigh over 200 pounds because they exhale too much carbon dioxide and cause air pollution!"

Holding back a student take-over of my lecture at the University of British Columbia in Vancouver.

Posing on the White House lawn with President Johnson's two dogs (left to right), Yuki and Blanca.

Dr. Bruce Spencer with his "secretary" lectures Westinghouse sales executives on the fallacy of creative thinking.

In the Press Room at the White House for the Lynda Bird Johnson—Charles Robb wedding.

Hoaxing the Master Hoaxer, Jim Moran, as Pierre Berton moderates on his Canadian television show.

"Put me in a room alone with you for two hours, Mr. Rock, and I'm sure I could convert you to my way of thinking!"

flying-plane passengers—were insane but apparently believable.

One particular account executive was enthusiastic in his desire for more details on my exciting announcement and he was ready to buy space on a thousand bald-headed men! When the hoax was revealed his jaw dropped and he sat stunned for the remainder of the meeting.

Over the years our paths have crossed a number of times and he always turns abruptly away, refusing to acknowledge my friendly nod.

When I was hired by the New York Chapter of the Sales Promotion Executives Association to address their members, only William J. Beardsley of *The National Observer*, Ron Rosenberg of Philip Morris, and Jack Moss, an independent film producer, were insiders. I was scheduled to speak at a special luncheon aboard the S.S. *Santa Paula* and the membership received this announcement about me in the mail:

> Dr. Bruce Spencer attended Ohio State University. Upon graduating with honors he received a private grant for a ten-year study in the fields of advertising and sales promotion. At the conclusion of his study, he had amassed over 10,000,000 words on paper, 5,000 miles of audio tape interviews and 25,000 graphs. Another grant from the same foundation permitted him an additional six years to analyze and evaluate his ten years of research. Dr. Bruce Spencer is presently associated with Confidential and Personality Profile, Ltd. (C&PP), a private firm that investigates employees in great depth entirely through the use of electronic devices.

The luncheon came off quite well and I gave them variations of my advertising flapdoodle that portrayed me as a sort of consultant, straightforward and rather immoral:

"You men are supposed to fashion your company's image through the muck and mire of the advertising jungle called 'competition.' But just how determined are you to succeed for your big boss? Are you willing to go to jail for him? Die for him? Perhaps even lose your job? I was recently called in by one of the largest used-car lots in Los Angeles to help their sagging sales; they had just dumped their sales promotion executive for spending too much time in the back seat of higher-priced models with female customers. The first thing I did to hypo their business was have them advertise a 1968 Oldsmobile for $99.99. We rigged the car so the radio played only when the car drove in reverse; the horn blew automatically when you used the brakes; green smoke that gushed out of the exhaust was linked up to the directional signals. And if anybody really wanted to drive that car off the lot, we could flatten all four tires by a remote radio signal in the office. Now this sort of sales promotion used to be known as 'bait advertising.' The Federal Trade Commission called it 'deceptive selling.' I like to refer to it as 'dramatic merchandising.' "

At the conclusion there was the same shock as always, some embarrassment, certainly the feeling they had been entertained, but by the most unusual "professional consultant" they had ever heard as the headlined speaker.

Jeanne assisted me at this affair by handling the charts and graphs. She played the bumbling secretary beautifully and I referred to her self-consciously as "my associate, my assistant—ah, Miss Smith." Whenever I rang my bell on the lectern for a change of charts, she would bring the wrong one out, put it on the easel upside down, knock over the easel or forget to perform when I rang for her attention. Much of the time she just looked longingly at me. The audience was certain we had some sort of a clandestine arrangement.

When I appeared as a guest speaker before the Philadelphia Television and Radio Advertising Club I startled them with ideas even more outrageous than before:

"The biggest fallacy behind creative thinking today is thinking you're being creative. There is no such thing as a 'new idea.' Even the Trojan horse was lifted from a band of Viking raiders who first sneaked into enemy ports aboard a ship shaped like a fake horse. Trying to think up original ideas can be frustrating. Especially if your mind is a blank. That's why I recommend borrowing a successful gimmick or thought from someone else—who probably stole it himself—change a little here and there, sign your own name and use it boldly. Nobody will ever be the wiser and you might even be lucky enough to earn credit as the originator!

"In today's business world nobody ever thinks twice about fishing around for other people's ideas and the best ones are generally found on scraps of paper under the boss's desk. Here is the content of one lucky piece I discovered after office hours that sent me up the ladder of success:

Darling F.J.:

Our little session behind the water cooler meant so much to me. When are you going to tell *Her*? I can't go on eating TV dinners alone just because you're married to *Her*. Please, dearest, tell *Her* you are mine.

Forever yours,
Tootsie

P.S. Forgive me for sending that letter to Westinghouse and signing it "love." But that's how distraught I am since the doctor told me about my condition.

"F.J. was chairman of the board. This original note plus one photostat copy and a little common sense gave me my first big break. He tripled my salary and sent me to the Chicago office as a vice-president in charge of vital statistics. Eventually F.J. got a divorce, married his secretary and fired me. So I went out on my own and became an advertising consultant, armed only with the motto of my college teacher, the late and great Professor Kutzmeier, who said: 'The shortest distance between two lies is the truth.' Well, this is hogwash, I found out. And the professor shot himself. He couldn't live, not with that kind of thinking. But we must go on in spite of such things.

"One of the big money drains on ad agencies concerns commercial jingles. By the time you get through paying a copywriter, musicians, studios, singers and production people you may have ten or fifteen thousand sunk into a one-minute radio spot. Why spend all this money when *anybody* can write a jingle, sing it themselves, record it at home and have it played directly to a studio for airing over the telephone! Total cost, not including airtime, $2.37.

"I've found that people on the street, amateur song writers and account executives' wives are eager to display their hidden talents. Often they don't want or expect payment: The free exposure is more than satisfying. And so my suggestion is to allow the simple housewife to contribute commercials; she has already demonstrated her ability to cook dinner, do the ironing, watch the kids and television simultaneously. Let her provide a jingle that uses public domain music—again saving on paying for the rights—and send her a case of the client's product for good will and to show you're a good sport.

"Here is a sample of one jingle that I recommended for Bloomingdale's. It's sung to the tune of 'London Bridge':

> *Bloomingdale's is marking down*
> *Marking down, marking down.*
> *Bloomingdale's is marking down*
> *For fair ladies.*

"That was created by the wife of a policeman. Here's one from the doorman of my apartment building. It's sung to 'Home on the Range':

> *Smooth, smooth, on the draw.*
> *Camels are good for the throat.*

"Very effective, wouldn't you say? Here's another one, in a classical vein from *The Mikado*, written by a frankfurter stand vendor right around the corner from here:

> *When the Dickie bird sang, oh what did he sing?*
> *Howard Johnson, Howard Johnson, Howard Johnson.*

"Now this is a very dramatic test. Notice that I have here a can of Ballantine beer alongside a can of Brand X. I'm going to strike this tuning fork and hold it on top of the Ballantine beer. Hear it? A perfect 440 'A' right in tune. Next I'll strike the tuning fork again and hold it on top of Brand X. Hear it? *This beer is flat!* Now this sort of television commercial doesn't make any sense at all. But that's why it's so powerful. Strong negative selling. The consumer actually *runs* to the corner store for his Ballantine beer."

This lecture was written up in *Television Age* by Don Dunn, presently assistant marketing editor for *Business*

Week. Dunn wrote a tongue-in-cheek but straight appraisal of my views under the heading: "Creativity is a four-letter word. . . . A new approach to the problem of building sales, as viewed by an unrecognized authority. . . . by Dr. Bruce Spencer." He ended his piece with my "Creative Recipe":

> "To one pound of imagination, add eight ounces of enthusiasm; stir in a cup of common sense, a pinch of audacity and two drops of irreverence; then add a pint of persistence and two quarts of courage. Mix these ingredients thoroughly, then simmer over a low fire for several hours. Let cool for at least a day before serving."

Ad man Stanley Elkman in Phadelphia saw through the spoof, but apparently one of his clients didn't.

> Dear Mr. Spencer:
>   One of our clients read about you in *Television Age* and took it very seriously since he believes most of the things you talk about. He refuses to believe that it is otherwise, even though we have tried to point out the "spoofing" that is involved.
>   Having a great deal of respect for your creative reputation, I would appreciate it if you found a few moments to drop me a line so that I can prove my point. Please come to the aid of some very creative advertising agency people.
>
>   Sincerely,
>   Stanley Elkman

I sent a notorized statement to Elkman swearing that he had judged me correctly.

A few days later I received a call from Arnold Silverman, a free-lance writer and friend, who reported overhearing a request for a copy of *The Fallacy of Creative Thinking* in a Madison Avenue bookstore. The customer didn't remember the name of the author and so Arnold supplied it for him, "Dr. Bruce Spencer." Imagine his surprise when the clerk said they had the book on order from their wholesaler because there had been a number of requests for it!

Then I received an urgent request from Emerson Foote, former chairman of the board of Foote, Cone & Belding Advertising, requesting a copy of my book, *The Fallacy of Creative Thinking*. When I didn't answer his letter right away there were several phone calls from his secretary to remind me that Mr. Foote was impatiently waiting for a copy of my book. He was willing to buy it; they just couldn't find it in any of the better book stores.

I sent this note of apology:

Dear Miss Fitzpatrick:

Thank you for your interest in obtaining a copy of my book *The Fallacy of Creative Thinking*. Since I now possess the only copy of this controversial treatise, I am a little reluctant to part with it. You see, the volatile nature of the subject matter has already instigated a number of legal actions against me, several threats of bodily harm, numerous hate letters and now I am permanently barred from a well-known yacht club my grandfather helped build.

Once my copy is passed around it starts people boiling because very few of us can live with the truth. Even I myself find it difficult at times.

So I trust you will not be too disappointed and extend my regrets to Mr. Foote over this matter.

Respectfully yours,
Bruce Spencer
Advertising Consultant

That was the last I heard from Mr. Foote's office, but there were other requests from people in the trade. And

Max W. Hahn, vice-president in charge of advertising for Avis Rent-a-Car, wrote me that he was forwarding my ideas on bald-head advertising to Doyle, Dane, Bernbach advertising for their review and consideration. And so it went.

One of my most responsive audiences was a party at the St. Regis Hotel given by Peters, Griffin, Woodward, Inc., a television-time sales organization representing more than forty-five stations around the country. As Dr. Bruce Spencer I took them down the primrose path with some new nonsense:

"I wonder how many of you heard the shocking news along advertising row today. The CBS conference room has been bugged for the past four months! Not by NBC or ABC but Radio Free Europe. And the State Department has issued their usual 'no comment.'

"So how can we improve the TV sales picture? Earn more dollars per viewer! One way is to use an integrated family commercial that promotes five different products in one minute! Imagine this living room scene: Father is sipping Gallo wine, Mother is eating Metrecal cookies. Grandma is taking her Ex-Lax, a teen-age daughter is using Scope for bad breath, and her twin brother is sniffing Elmer's Glue—to provide a touch of humor. This is real powerful on TV, what I call a blockbuster throwaway, a dramatic loss leader.

"I also recommend that a sponsor slip in a few frames from a nudie film during his one-minute commercial. That's only an eye blink, ladies, nothing to blush about really. But the 'did-I-see-what-I-saw!' effect on viewers sure moves a lot of products off the shelves. We tested it in

Kalamazoo last month—four frames from Bob Downey's sensational underground film *No More Excuses,* where the chimp gets in bed with the girl—with Mennin's Baby Powder. They sold out in twenty-four hours!

"Another sure-fire winner is the 'hunchback' commercial. For instance we show a man eating a Sara Lee pie with a Heinz pickle and then he washes this mixture down with a glass of Alka Seltzer. This man gets mighty sick on camera. It's what we call negative selling. Nobody ever, ever forgets the products."

By the time I had reached my question and answer section with this audience, they were more than certain I had been pulling their collective legs. Yet they seemed to enjoy the presentation as much, if not more, than other groups who were never sure until they had been told.

"What was perhaps your most famous achievement, Dr. Spencer?" asked George Castleman, a vice-president of Peters, Griffin, Woodward and one of the men responsible for my appearance.

I thought for a moment, snapped my fingers as though I had just remembered, and then invented some more flapdoodle: "When was the last time you heard of a television station going bankrupt? I'll give you an inside story how I helped save a station from folding. Confidentially, it was KTTV out in Los Angeles. They were on the rocks —I won't say when—and management called me in. They said they needed money, a lot of cash, immediately, to meet the month's payroll. Among others they had Joe Pyne and he wasn't working for peanuts! This was on a Friday. By Monday, through my intervention, they were solvent again.

"Over the weekend I hired an oil rig, set it up in their parking lot and started to dig for oil. We had four uniformed policemen to keep away the crowds. Wild rumors spread all over Hollywood that KTTV struck oil. We said nothing. Within twelve hours there were twenty-two offers to buy the parking lot for one hundred times its value. A very astute real estate investor from San Francisco finally bought the land by phone, sight unseen. And then he rented it back to the station for a dollar a year, keeping only the mineral rights. This man drilled for something like three months. I think he went straight down almost two miles. Nothing but mud and rock. But again, business is business. I saved a near bankruptcy—and received my usual 25 per cent commission off the top."

Through word of mouth, Dr. Bruce Spencer earned a reputation for his ability to shake up a dull sales meeting. Few people ever recognized me from one appearance to another because I used different material, sometimes wore a disguise and—if challenged—denied being anybody but myself, whoever that was at the time.

In January, 1969, Jeanne and I appeared before the yearly meeting of all Dow Jones circulation sales managers. As a private circulation consultant, with Jeanne as my inept helper, I proceeded to hammer away at them:

"Your boss, Bill Kerby, told me to go out and get the facts and to spare no expense because Dow Jones publications are in deep trouble. My team did a survey in Mineral City, Ohio. Seventy-eight per cent of the respondents there never heard of *The Wall Street Journal*; 21 per cent asked, 'What street was *that*?' And one citizen had our researcher arrested for loitering.

"We tested *The National Observer* before a select

group of Jehovah's Witnesses. They thought it was a house organ for a national nudist colony.

"To create a better image for *The Wall Street Journal* I've suggested that the daily stock quotations be printed in Hebrew and Latin symbols—to better relations with minority groups. And for the black community, I've recommended that we print the number of the day on Page One.

"When I spoke to clairvoyant Jeanne Dixon last summer she predicted *The Wall Street Journal* would live for another 200 years—no, that was *The Saturday Evening Post*. She gave *The Journal* 362 years.

"This fall you're going to see a lot more television advertising by *The Wall Street Journal*. At my suggestion the commercials will be performed by former political candidates who lost. Subliminally everybody likes to identify with a loser. How else could the *Daily News* remain number one in circulation? Or Ed Sullivan stay on the tube so many years? Remember Bill Miller? After he lost the bid for vice-president in 1964 he did a series of funeral-home commercials on TV. Their business went up 22 per cent. Just imagine how effective it would be to see General Curtis LeMay in uniform with a copy of *The Wall Street Journal* in one hand and a flame thrower in the other!

"*Barron's* will sponsor a new weekly television series entitled 'Life Inside Cuba.' Pilots from Eastern and National Airlines have been signed to tell their stories after being hijacked to Havana. And *The National Observer* will pick up the tab for an hour special on crime in the streets this summer. This is going to be an actual battle between the Black Panthers and the Hell's Angels, followed by live on-the-spot looting in downtown Chicago.

Mayor Daley will M.C. Some of the participating sponsors are Pittsburgh Plate Glass, the makers of Mace and Harley-Davidson Motorcycles."

The circulation sales managers responded with laughter throughout the thirty-five minute spoof and were in doubt about me only until I introduced my charts. The "lack of sales incentives" chart showed a curve that vaguely resembled a limp penis; the "sales incentives applied" chart suggested its excited counterpart.

However, another time, these charts and a *double entendre* question ("Does opera singer Maria Callas use her diaphragm?") that I used for a Westinghouse presentation caused some flack. Jeanne and I wrote and performed a half-hour advertising spoof on video tape for producer Jack Agnew to be shown at the National Association of Broadcasters convention in Chicago. When the Westinghouse brass saw the first screening in their New York offices they were furious over the inclusion of this "blue" material and stormed out of the conference room in protest, even though the salesmen and secretaries present loved it.

To my surprise it was shown in Chicago—again to an enthusiastic audience—and an NBC executive tried to beg, borrow or steal a print for his people. But he was too late. The tape was quickly sent to WBZ-TV in Boston, where it was quietly erased.

Nevertheless, Westinghouse employed my services on numerous occasions. At one of their national meetings in Cleveland I was hired to mingle with the four hundred or so guests and find fault with them. I was so successful that when it came time for dinner in the grand ballroom nobody would sit at my table. It must have been a weird sight for the waiters to see sixty or seventy tables, each filled to capacity, and there I was all alone at a table set for eight.

Afterwards I made a short speech complaining about the lack of imagination in Group W television programing (I wanted Adam Clayton Powell to host a new version of *To Tell the Truth*). And when I charged that the Group W logo suspiciously resembled the Volkswagen insignia, Vice-President Mitchell Benson had to be physically restrained from coming over and hitting me in the mouth. The Westinghouse people who did know me from prior experiences played dumb and secretly enjoyed every minute of my insult comedy.

I was revealed as a "professional hoaxer" when a special pilot film was shown with Mike Douglas and the Smothers Brothers trying to dress a donkey, and Gypsy Rose Lee holding a debate with me on "the indecency of naked animals."

Another time when I was physically threatened was during a private party at John Galbraith's Darby Dan retreat near Columbus, Ohio. A number of people from advertising, radio, television and industry were there to bid farewell to David Lewis, an executive with KDKA-TV in Pittsburgh who was being transferred to New York. Bob Novak, program manager at the station, and Tad Reeves, president of WBC Productions in New York, conspired to have me appear as a slightly drunken friend of Galbraith's who just happened to be in town. Then I was to set about causing trouble—saying the wrong thing at the wrong time, complaining about the food, service, décor and the Pittsburgh Pirates, owned by John Galbraith.

Several hundred elegantly dressed guests were talking quietly in the sumptuous Darby Dan den when I brazenly rang the doorbell that Saturday evening. I loudly announced my presence to the butler and brushed by him to greet the surprised people.

"Hey, what's going on here? A party! Wow! Show me to the bar quick! And where the hell are the girls? Hi, everybody. John Galbraith! Why you old buzzard, why didn't you let me know there was going to be a blast tonight? I would have brought a few of the boys along. Tad Reeves, of all people, don't tell me you brought your wife!!!"

From that moment on I had my nose in everybody's drink and conversation. I was the perfect pest. Dressed in a baggy suit, an open shirt and carrying an empty flask, I was a sight for sore eyes.

But Novak and Reeves pulled a switch on me. They had planted another ringer, actor-comedian Sterling Yates, who also played an insulting drunk. I thought he was for real most of the evening and avoided him as much as possible. But Yates kept getting in my way a little too often and this made me suspicious. One of his favorite stunts was to aim a fist in my direction from across the room and charge at me. Novak and Reeves managed to grab him just in time. The first two times I was prepared to duck, or throw a quick punch and run for my life.

The exposé was revealed around midnight just before a splendid dinner and everybody breathed a long, long sigh of relief. Fortunately, there had been a good many laughs, and the barbs were delivered with a sense of satire that never turned sour. It helped, too, that David Lewis and the other guests, not to mention host John Galbraith, were good sports.

THIRTEEN

THE JONES UNDERWEAR LETTERS

My company trade name used to be Bell Productions. At one time there was also a company in New York named Bell Products. They made advertising novelties and specialty items for large manufacturers as premium merchandise. I didn't know the other company existed until many months after I had an exchange of letters with the advertising manager of a clothing manufacturer I shall call the Jones Corporation. It all began when I received this communication the latter part of 1966:

> Alan Abel
> Bell Productions
> 507 Fifth Avenue
> New York, N.Y.
> Dear Sir:
>   Our 1967 advertising is being merchandised as "T-N-T" advertising to the trade.

N.W. Ayer has used a paper cylinder decorated as a piece of dynamite during a recent ad presentation and has given me your name as a possible supplier of this type of paper specialty.

What do you have that could be made to look like a firecracker or stick of dynamite. We're thinking of an item with a metal bottom and base, 3"–4" thick . . . 8"–10" high. Quantities: 500–1000.

Do you have stock items of this nature we can see?

Sincerely,
Advertising Manager
Jones Corporation

My first thought was that some joker at N.W. Ayer Advertising knew my reputation for pulling people's legs and wanted me to spoof his client. So I wrote the following reply:

Advertising Manager
Jones Corporation
1801 Avenue of the Americas
New York, N. Y.

Dear Sir:

Thank you for your letter. I would suggest your using a 60 mm shell casing made of cardboard with a wicker base that was once part of the Japanese arsenal on Okinawa.

These casings were removed to Hong Kong after the war and have been painted a bright red, white and blue by the labor force there, thus keeping the cost per piece down to an amazing low fee for a carload.

There is, of course, no danger of explosion as the powder has been removed along with the fuses. We have also used the official Chinese trade mark, "Made in U.S.A.," in order to conform to our standards for handling only merchandise that is sold American.

Each shell casing stands three feet high and is fourteen inches in diameter, making an excellent display that can be seen dramatically by people with the worst possible vision.

I'm sure you will be pleased with this revolutionary point-of-sale display casing and we look forward to serving your needs.

                    Respectfully yours,
                    Alan Abel

I received a reply as follows:

Dear Mr. Abel:

Thank you for your letter about the 60 mm shell casing that was once part of the Japanese arsenal on Okinawa.

This item sounds like the thing we need, but I am a little concerned about the price. We only need 500. What would be your quotation for 500?

                    Sincere regards,
                    Advertising Manager
                    Jones Corporation

P.S. Do you have an inexpensive item we might consider purchasing for "giveaways" in a Children's Wear Department store promotion . . . something suitable for a 5 or 6 year old child?

At this point I suspected that the adman was taking me rather seriously. I decided to answer more boldly, with several wild suggestions that would clue him I was pulling his leg.

Dear Sir:

I thought I would dash off a quick letter to you before leaving on a four-day skiing journey to Squaw Valley. The 60 mm Japanese shell casing, which we call the "Boomerang," is packed one hundred to a crate and now wholesales for $398.00 or $3.98 each.

I say "now" because the price jumped 87 per cent since my last letter to you. This increase was the result of a wildcat sitdown strike by several thousand coolies. You would think these smart alecs knew which side their rice patties were buttered on; many of them are from Japan, a nation we could have enslaved after World War II; but instead we let them compete freely with our world trade and then they stick us in the rear.

Well, I didn't mean to go off on this philosophical tangent, but it does burn me up. Then today we get word that one of the ships bringing us several thousand crates of "Boomerangs" sank off Johnson Island with a total loss including the crew. Not even the Captain was saved and they carried no insurance.

As to your request for kiddie giveaways. We do have another import from Java that is out of this world. It's a paper doll that wets. Not a lot; just enough, though, to keep the item self-liquidating and bring the youngsters back for more. It's a stand-up colored miniature in 3-D that weighs only four ounces. They come in lots of 1200 and sell for $300 a lot.

> Sincerely,
> Alan Abel

Dear Mr. Abel:

Thank you very much for your letter. Things have got to get better . . . perhaps some of the "Boomerangs" which sank off Johnson Island will float to the surface and be recovered.

I sure appreciate your interest in finding us a giveaway for a children's wear store promotion. The paper doll from Java which you mentioned is quite expensive for our budget. Do you have anything in the price range of 10-20 cents each?

> Sincerely yours,
> Adman

Dear Adman:

My apologies for the long delay in answering your letter, however, I decided to take a trip to Europe to see if we couldn't come up with something really attractive for you people. And I do believe we have the perfect item for Jones Corporation!

But first let me say that "Boomerangs" are out of style. So it's just as well that you never got stuck with them. And, as you may remember, we lost a boatload in the South Pacific. Good riddance! Believe it or not, the damn coolies are still on strike, squatting along the riverbank picking their toenails in between U.S. servicemen washings.

After spending a month in France and taking a lot of muck from the natives (they still blame America for their losing to the Nazis because a U.S. contractor built the Maginot Line! Such idiocy*), I found a wind-up frog that grunts, croaks, spits, swallows and dives. But the inventor wanted me to buy not only the patent but also find a mistress for him in Omaha, Nebraska. Seems like he visited there twenty years ago and met a nice waitress. Now he thinks only nice people come from Omaha. So I lost him and his kind in a hurry.

Then I took a trip to Egypt as I promised the little woman some photos of the pyramids. Wouldn't you know it, I got lost in the desert, the camel I rented for a week died the second day out, and some Arab rascal I hired as my guide took all my clothes one night along with my wallet! The only thing he left me was my Hanes underwear I had on and a $50 bill I always sleep with under my right armpit.

Well, Mr. Adman, I don't want to bore you with all my troubles when I haven't even let you in on the greatest giveaway item in the history of retail merchandising. Here it is (something that happened quite accidentally when I hitchhiked on a goat going to Cairo—for $50) : I checked into the Cairo Hilton and they thought I was a native in my underwear and the suntan. So I had no trouble without baggage. By staying in my room and signing the checks for all meals brought up, I was able to wait out a cable from the States with sufficient money to start being a human again. It was at that moment that I hit on this premium item.

In actuality it was the Israel-Arab war. The day was June 4, the day before the attack. I was on the balcony with binoculars watching the women go down to the River Nile for their morning constitutional. They were also carrying their husbands' *white robes*.

Well, that did it. I figured I could do something with the white robes, actually sheets. So I hit the market place at El Zebe A Rheme and found that I could not only buy all the sheets I wanted but they could be cut to any size.

To make this long letter short, within a week the war was lost and just about every Arab soldier had lost his sheet if not his life or his b — — — s. My contact in the market was able to pick up 150,000 sheets from the women who dropped them in a dash for the safety of the hills.

We had these sheets cleaned at the riverbank by small boys who were doing nothing but begging anyhow; then they were cut to 1 foot squares and I have as of this writing been notified by Maurice Shieb, my agent in Cairo, that 1,000,230 squares of sheet are en route to our warehouse in New Jersey.

My offer to you, my dear sir, is a premium of one million pieces of sheet to be advertised as 100 per cent genuine Arab. Every man, woman and child in America would want to be the proud owner of a piece of Arab sheet, as a collector's item.

Our charge to you would be one cent each or $10,000 for the lot. Keep in mind this item is perfectly useless, just a gimmick, but a valuable merchandising gesture to take advantage of the recent war in the Middle East.

Furthermore, to keep good relations, you can advise customers that the net profits will go to a good cause. We plan to donate at least $2000 to the Red Cross from this business venture and, hopefully, they will be able to sell us some of their Red sheets. But that's another deal. More later. I await your good word.

Sincerely yours,
Alan Abel

Dear Mr. Abel:

Although we are not able to purchase the one million sheet squares as you suggested in your letter of July 31, I do want to thank you for keeping us in mind and bringing me up to date on your recent activities.

Please don't hesitate to let me know when you think you have an item you feel we can use in our sales promotion program.

Sincerely,
Advertising Manager
Jones Corporation

There was still some doubt in my mind as to whether Adman now knew it was a gag or thought I was completely insane. So I sent him a note that explained things and enclosed a copy of one of my books spoofing advertising, with a friendly inscription. But I never heard from the Jones Corporation again.

FOURTEEN

JULIUS BRISTOL
GOLF PRO

My wife and I were visiting the Trapp Family Lodge in Stowe, Vermont, back in February of 1966. During the second day of our stay I decided to try out a compass Jeanne had given me and we soon found ourselves lost in the woods. After wandering in circles on our snowshoes, her homing instinct finally brought us back to the lodge.

The snow was great, and the sun. We were enjoying ourselves. But, as it never fails to happen when we go away for a few days, there was an urgent phone message to call New York City. Milt Shefter, sales promotion manager for Westinghouse broadcasting stations, was on the other end of the line.

"I don't know if you remember me, Mr. Abel, but you insulted me in Cleveland during the Westinghouse convention last year. And I've been meaning to tell you how much I enjoyed it."

I was relieved to learn that Shefter hadn't taken offense as had so many others during that particular assignment.

"Have you ever played golf?" he asked.

"Only twice," I said. "Once at the Denver Country Club about twenty years ago. On my first try I hit the ball at a right angle and smacked an elderly lady in the middle of her upswing. She came after me and I took off for the clubhouse. You might call that my 'one stroke' game. The only other time was at the Lake Tarleton Club in New Hampshire five years ago. I went nine holes in 198 strokes and lost three balls. That's when I quit the game for good."

"Fine," said Shefter. "You're just the man I need."

He then went on to explain that I was to pose as a professional golf pro for the National Association of Broadcasters' convention to be held in Chicago during the last week of March. My base of operations would be the Westinghouse suite at the Hotel Hilton, where a temporary golf green would be laid and I could teach my craft—with a serious demeanor but using satirical techniques.

After I agreed to play golf pro for three days (using the pseudonym of "Julius Bristol from the Philippines") I began to have second thoughts. The men I would be instructing were all enthusiastic golfers who had spent years at the game and many were practically pros themselves. How could I convince them I was a champion when I had held the clubs only twice in my life?

Since I had but three weeks in which to work up my routine, we returned to New York from Vermont several days earlier than planned. Then I scoured the bookstores for manuals on golfing and bought a dozen authoritative books by Gary Player, Sam Sneed, Arnold Palmer and others. If I knew nothing else, at least I recognized the names of these champions!

After staying up nights reading each book from cover to cover, I became more confused about the game than ever. None of the pros were in agreement on the little things, like whether a No. 5 wood was easier and more dependable than a No. 3 iron. To me, an outsider, it seemed strange there was no singularly correct approach. Fortunately, the common confusion of the pros was going to work in my favor.

The week before the convention I memorized golfing phrases: "This is a honey of an approach . . . your back swing and down swing are critical . . . right on the lip . . . use the No. 6 iron for a second shot . . . put those three-footers out."

Jeanne taught me various ballet positions because I intended to use them for improving the putting stance. And I already had my four hundred dollar costume from Abercrombie & Fitch, complete with a multicolored blazer, red pants, yellow shirt, tan ascot, straw hat and a slightly warped putter—which I never intended to use if I could help it!

Just for insurance—in the event somebody important insisted I play a round of golf—I bought an arm sling in a medical supply store so I could pretend to have a broken arm. Away I went to Chicago.

The N.A.B. convention was a beehive of activity with more than five thousand radio and television executives in attendance. I taught several hundred of them golf—everybody from the president of a television station chain (he even invited me aboard his yacht on Lake Michigan) down to time salesmen. And I was taken quite seriously. The only people who knew I was a fake were Milt Shefter; his boss, Jack Rhodes; and the president of Westinghouse Productions, Les Arries. They were naturally delighted to see me teach VIPs from the broadcasting industry, whom they all knew, how to putt while standing on point!

Coincidentally, the Seven Arts–Warner Brothers television exhibit at the Hilton also had a golf pro—a real one by the name of Pete Mazzetta, who was with the Holland Park Country Club in Chicago. When word about Julius Bristol started going around, along with my revolutionary methods for playing, some bright fellow suggested that Mazzetta and Bristol should hold a putting match. I discouraged any such thoughts.

Up until the afternoon of my second day I had been able to avoid hitting the ball. I just gave instructions, helped people with their grips, held their arms while they stood on their toes and offered all kinds of encouragement.

Peter E. Schruth, vice-president for the Group W Stations, was a weekend golfer who asked me for a tip or two. I gave him the full treatment:

"Drop your left shoulder a bit, sir. We've got to compensate for the angle of the club, especially on a downhill line bunker shot. Now spread your toes, that's it, lean forward; don't concentrate on the ball yet—that's not important—steady now—hold your breath. . . ."

I had the poor guy so confused, standing there all twisted up, I finally urged him to "take a shot and let's get it over with." I blinked in amazement as he made a hole-in-one. And so did he!

The unlucky people who received a few pointers from Julius Bristol also earned free golf balls—with a choice of either Merv Griffin's or Mike Douglas' autograph—and a handful of brightly colored tees embossed with "Julius Bristol—Golf Pro." There were handouts that explained my Perfect Putting Posture was the necessary ballet positions diagrammed for the feet. I gave away thousands of personally autographed photographs showing me holding a $35,000 check that was supposedly issued by the Quezon City Bank of Manila and signed by T.J. Manuel, President of the Philippine Golf Tournament. All these names were fictitious, of course.

On the back of my souvenir photograph a short biographical sketch explained:

> For the past ten years the name Julius Bristol has been as well known in the Philippines as Arnold Palmer or Sam Snead is in the States. He has the distinct honor of having made three holes-in-one and he is the first $35,000 winner of the 1963 Manila Open Golf Tournament.*
>
> At one time or another the top ten golfers in the United States have agreed unanimously that Julius is one of the most underrated and least understood professionals in the business. His *Perfect Putting Posture* technique for achieving 89% accuracy on the green has been published around the world in twelve languages. Thousands of weekend golfers now swear by it.
>
> MR. BRISTOL ENDORSES FOOT-JOY GOLF SHOES
>
> * NOTE: The 1963 Manila Open Golf Tournament was held only once and subsequent tournaments were canceled due to the bickering among local golf officials concerning improper handling of treasury funds. Meantime, the 1963 sterling silver winning trophy sits in Julius Bristol's den and he has invested most of his $35,000 purse in twelve self-service shoe shine stands on Manila's main streets.

Larry Carino, general manager of WJBK-TV in Detroit,

took a ballet lesson from me while struggling with his putter. Then he insisted that I demonstrate the superiority of my Perfect Putting Posture. It was too late for me to pretend I had a broken arm—I had discarded the sling on arrival, figuring it was too much of a cop-out—so there was only one thing for me to do: play golf for the third time in twenty years.

Quite a crowd gathered around to watch me and I took my time in lining up the ball and taking practice swings. I held my breath, closed my eyes and gave the ball a hard whack down the twenty-foot green toward the hole. It went straight in! The room rocked with cheers and applause. I shook hands all around.

Now professional golfer Pete Mazzetta entered the suite and challenged me to a match. I was about to face the moment of truth. Nearly a hundred people crowded around us and our conversation went something like this:

PETE: Let's flip a coin to see who goes first.

JULIUS: Why don't you just go ahead and shoot?

PETE: No, I want to be fair about this.

JULIUS: No you don't. I think you just want to win. So go ahead, I'll just watch. I don't feel competitive right now. After all, I'm here to teach, not to play games. . . .

PETE: Well, I'll go ahead and try four balls, O.K.?

JULIUS: Sure, why not. But keep in mind that I haven't had any sleep the past two nights, my legs and arms are tired from instructing twelve hours a day, so don't expect too much from me.

Mazzetta hit four bulls-eyes, one right after another. I lined up my first shot, started a slow-motion swing, hesitated, stopped and put down my club to test the floor with a carpenter's level. Next I sprayed the club head with insect repellent "to keep away the flies" and chalked the edge as though I were playing billiards instead of golf.

I continued with other ridiculous preshooting activities while keeping a perfectly straight face. Pete Mazzetta had begun to laugh and couldn't stop. I ignored him. The onlookers registered various degrees of interest, amusement and confusion.

Using a tape measure I spotted my ball on a straight line with the hole, double-checked my position with a pool bridge, dusted the green with a whisk broom and then sprayed the path between my ball and the hole with more insect repellent. So far I had spent ten minutes preparing and the crowd was getting restless. They began urging me to shoot.

"You fellows in the rear are ruining my game!" I shouted to several Westinghouse salesmen who were serving drinks and talking business. "I must have absolute silence or I will not shoot."

As the room noise quieted down I began wrist warm-up exercises and I flailed my arms around. Mazzetta was still laughing and I heard him remark to someone: "I've been from Maine to Spain and never have seen anything like this guy. He's a human helicopter!"

I laid down all four balls, hit each one in quick succession and watched them bunch up at the hole without scoring a single point. Pete Mazzetta was the winner hands down and I congratulated him. He was still laughing when he left the room. My rapid-fire shots had not fooled Mazzetta, but apparently many of the watchers were taken in.

Outside the Westinghouse suite, in front of the elevators, a smartly dressed executive had his putter and was practicing ballet position no. 2 in front of a full-length hall mirror. At the moment I saw him, he took a swing, and lost his balance, fell over on the carpet and almost broke his putter.

Both Jack Rhodes and Milt Shefter were concerned that I had been too convincing; funny, yes, but so many executives were falling for this flapdoodle, it might cause hard feelings if I continued the farce much longer and the word got out I was an imposter. Originally they had planned to spill the beans on the final day of the convention, but this now seemed unwise.

So I was to give one final lesson the morning of the third day. Ten prospects were eagerly waiting for me when I showed up at 10 A.M. swinging my warped club.

"All right gentlemen," I said. "Assume ballet position no. 1 if you weigh less than 160 pounds and are under five feet six inches. Like this. If you weigh more than 160 pounds and are over five feet six inches tall, assume ballet position no. 2. Like this. These positions should give you minimum foot balance and anchor your weight for a simulated pendulum putt. Next, take a tight all-finger grip on your putter and focus your eyes on separate blades of grass on either side of the ball. *Do not look directly at the ball.* Instead, concentrate on two vertical grass blades as though you're looking through a stereopticon. Then you will see the ball dead-center between two fixed points. Take a deep breath. *Now hold it!* Try to relax. Next swing your putter quickly with confidence, using a steady wrist action. At the precise moment of impact with the ball, *exhale.* Let the putter continue a forward swing through an eight-inch arc to provide a slight touch of top spin. Ready. *Go!*

"As soon as you retrieve the balls that went out into the hallway, let's try once again. While we're waiting, those of you who didn't lose their balls, practice your putting with me. Get ready—toes on their mark—stand on point—concentrate—inhale—swing—exhale!"

Two hours later I was on a nonstop jet back to New York. A month later *Television Age* cautiously suggested a hoax with an article headed "The Great Putt On" that said:

> Station executives around the country have been seen in some curious postures ever since the NAB Convention, shuffling about on the carpets of their offices and prancing like Chaplin with toes pointing out in ballet positions. What they're doing is practicing a new putting stance, taught to them at the Chicago Convention by a flamboyant golf pro named Julius Bristol, who gave lessons in the WBC Program Sales suite.
>
> Toffishly dressed in the most modish golfing attire, Mr. Bristol lightened his lessons in Perfect Putting Posture with shenanigans with the new model putter he was testing, by sandpapering the leading edge and spraying it.
>
> Although Mr. Bristol lost a putting match to a golf pro from the Seven Arts' suite, his verbal expertise in minutiae of golf and locker-room activities from Tasmania to Mindanao amazed conventioneers.
>
> After the convention a WBC Program Sales executive named Milt Shefter tried to pull a hoax, claiming that 'Julius Bristol' did not exist, but was an actor named Alan Abel. The conventioneers snorted at the attempt.

The February, 1967, issue of the *Golf Digest Annual* devoted a full page to my stunt under the heading "Hoax of the Year." They said in part:

> If this spring while waiting your turn to tee off you notice that the golfer ahead of you has planted his feet in a seemingly unorthodox way—say with his heels together and his feet pointing due north and south—don't be surprised. The

man has been taking lessons from 1966's non-playing pro of the year, Julius Bristol, a professional impostor.

Few saw through Bristol's act, even when he announced the Manila Open had been canceled after his win in 1963 because of financial chicanery on the part of tournament officials, or when he sprayed his putter with insect repellent to keep away the flies.

At least one TV station manager at the convention tried out Bristol's ballet stance No. 1 and said with conviction: "It's unusual, but I'll try anything to help my game."

Only this past year, while I was addressing a meeting of television station representatives in New York, I admitted the farce that took place in Chicago. One executive leaped to his feet and shouted excitedly, "My God! I took lessons from you and my game actually *improved!*"

FIFTEEN

TAKING
ON THE BRITISH

From what I'd heard, Speaker's Corner in London's
Hyde Park is a great place to visit. I was pleased, therefore, when the Canadian Broadcasting Company encouraged me to go there and speak so they could film the occasion Candid Camera style. The CBC offered to share
expenses for my wife and me in England in exchange for
a half-hour television documentary.

Speaker's Corner is at one corner of Hyde Park beside
a familiar landmark, the great Marble Arch, which used
to be the site of public hangings a few centuries back.
But now all sorts of rascals have free reign there. They
come regularly to entertain, provoke, discourse. And
much of the audience comes regularly as well.

This mental sport seems peculiarly common to the

English and for all the shouting and general madness that goes on at Speaker's Corner, the crowds are generally well mannered and polite. In America, if a man is on a soapbox, he's promoting civil disobedience or inciting a riot; in London, soapbox oratory is sporting and an institution. The only rules are those forbidding insults directed at the Queen and open insurrection.

Upon our arrival Jeanne and I wandered from speaker to speaker. Several preachers spoke from elaborate platforms that were collapsible and portable. One spoke so meekly it was hard to hear what he had to say. His sign said he represented the Protestant Truth Society. Another speaker, a stout woman, led passersby in lusty singing while a small boy danced. A young girl spoke on behalf of the Hyde Park Tories. Another man with tattoos all over his face and bald head stripped to the waist to reveal more tattoos on his chest, back and arms as well. A strange little man in knickers stood quietly on a piano stool and mutely held his sign aloft: "That Ye Love One Another." "God Is Love" was lettered on the vest of a hippie as he strolled through the crowds. And a little lady who must have been a hundred years old promised that "you can develop the power to see God with your own physical eyes in just seven days if you joined the 'Universal Occult-Divine Order' immediately."

Some speakers were not so benign. Since the Arab-Israeli War of June, 1967, had just ended, there was some very heated speechmaking. The bobbies were there to keep order with only their dignity as a weapon. When one Arab speaker got so excited he was threatened by an Israeli in the crowd, the bobby quietly reminded the challenger: "I say now, the speaker has a right to his opinion, doesn't he?"

I chose an area near a man who was so emotional in his diatribe you couldn't understand a word. His sign said: "The Time Is Short" and this stimulated thought. But only five or six people were attracted to his soapbox.

I took my own place in the melee. I was dressed in red slacks, a Madras jacket and brown ascot, with flashy medals (I had bought them in an antique shop) dangling heavily from my breast pocket. The crew for the Canadian Broadcasting Corporation, with some help from the BBC, had set up their equipment unobtrusively and I had secreted a microphone in my shirt pocket.

My first problem was to attract a crowd. So I stepped up on a wooden crate that appropriately enough carried the brand name of an English beverage—'Courage.'

"The earth is moving!" I shouted to meandering strollers.

"Hey, Mabel. Here's another one," I heard an American tourist tell his wife as they gravitated toward me. Others followed while I continued talking.

"A top scientist has revealed to me that the earth is rapidly spinning into another solar system."

"An' who might this scientist be?" a frog-eyed fellow asked.

"I'm not at liberty to reveal such top-secret information," I countered. "But you can take it from me he's a cautious man. He always wipes his silverware in restaurants, he pays income tax on gifts he receives at Christmas."

As more and more people gathered around to listen I explained the cause of our earth's accelerated movement. "We're walking too fast, driving too fast. And all this trampling and pushing, as dashing commuters in speeding cars rush to and from work, is adding inertia to the earth's forward motion. Like the top spin on a tennis player's ball. It is a known fact that a person is heavier when he's tired. But nowadays, we have so many labor-saving devices that people don't get as tired. So, with less tired blood there's not enough body ballast to maintain the earth's gravity. Electric pencil sharpeners and electric can openers my be the ruination of us all!"

"Hey, mate!" shouted a young Cockney. "You American, right?"

"How could you tell?" I replied, at which everyone had a good English laugh.

"Why don't you go back there?" he asked again.

"And take you with me?" I replied quickly, as the crowd again laughed. "You'd like that, but first you better help your country pay up its war debts. Uncle Sam still hasn't forgotten—"

"The United States could never have started in the first place without the Bank of England!" a woman interrupted angrily.

"Lady," I said, "you're just jealous because we did so well for ourselves since the Boston Tea Party!"

By this time I had taken onlookers from the tattooed man and the angry, long-winded fellow whose time was so short. The professional hecklers pushed their way up front so they could go to work on me. The bobbies had forgotten the Arab momentarily and sauntered around my audience, now growing in size, smiling to themselves as they listened to this newcomer from America. The cameras were rolling again after a change of film.

"Now you take the jet engine on a plane. I'm very suspicious of it and I think it's a hoax. There's nothing in there to make it go. Those so-called 'jet engines' are decoys! They're just hi-fi speakers for the announcements and the music. And the real power is actually back in the ladies' room!"

"Yeah, man," said a hippie in a serape.

"That's why I suggest we *each* fly—each under his own power. I am referring to a new discovery that will enable us to grow wings from our shoulder blades." Titters ran through the crowd and people edged in closer to me. "Once we had tails—"

"I think I'll have a piece of one right now," interrupted the hippie as he left.

"But," I continued, "we lost them in the process of evolution because they were uncomfortable to sit on. Sit on a rope for five minutes, if you need convincing. So why is it so hard to imagine that our bodies can't grow wings? Think of the convenience to fly yourself—no more plane reservations, expenses or holding patterns!"

"Can you fly away?" asked a heckler.

"Sir, you laughed at the Wright Brothers too, didn't you? Well, I have started to learn to fly myself. Unfortunately, I'm afraid I can't demonstrate for you today because I had a little accident last New Year's Eve—"

"You landed on your head," came a voice from the crowd.

"No, I flew out a second-floor window. And it felt exhilarating for a few seconds. But then something must have gone wrong, because the next thing I knew I had crash-landed on the umbrella of a closed frankfurter stand."

There were now at least two or three hundred people trying to get close enough to hear and I was straining my voice to reach those on the outer edges of the crowd.

"Once you people learn to fly I'd like to recruit a colony for a trip to the moon. Think of the advantages up there. You won't find any smog. Traffic noises are unheard of—"

"Why not?" asked a voice.

"Because there's no traffic," I answered. "And this means no highway accidents—thereby increasing your life expectency by ten years and cutting your accident insurance premiums by 50 per cent."

"But I don't drive," someone offered.

"But *they* do!" I replied, pointing to the many Austin-Healey taxicabs that spun around the corner of the park, their air pollution contributing to the hazy smog that always seemed to hover over London.

"What's your opinion on the war?" asked a ruddy-faced fellow down front.

"I have inside information that the recent Arab-Israeli war was staged by J. Arthur Rank for a motion picture film. Yes, that's right. The producer had a one-week shooting schedule and he made it right on time."

This outrageous statement was met with scattered laughs and many guffaws.

"You don't believe me?" I countered. "Then listen to any Arab radio report on the war. They say they won. Then listen to any Israeli report. They say they won. I say J. Arthur Rank won! He's got all the action down on film and will make millions on it. You just wait and see."

At this time the Arab speaker joined my crowd and expressed annoyance over the whimsy of my comments. He was genuinely upset. A tall, muscular bobby moved in close to the Arab and just cleared his throat. That was all. The Arab disappeared.

"Wars are stupid, anyhow," I continued. "If we would use children to fight, it would be simply a matter of arming them with toy guns and water pistols. They love to fight and habitually play at war games. Why not allow them to settle all our adult quarrels in such a harmless manner? Need I mention the savings in military spending? And the country with the most little soldiers left wins the war."

"Next you'll be telling us that Adolf Hitler is alive," spoke a heckler from somewhere in the back. It so happened that I had prepared some material on this provocative thought and he couldn't have made a better introduction for me.

"Adolf is not only alive and well, he runs a little drive-in diner near the Swiss border—naturally I'm not at liberty to say where—and I recently asked him what the real motive was behind his dastardly deeds. He said bitterly that it had all started in Austria in the early twenties when, as a struggling artist, he had tried to sell his paintings on the sidewalk. Then one day an Englishman said that Hitler's water color of Big Ben was a piece of rubbish. Well, my friend, we have that Englishman to blame for what happened to the world after that!"

After three hours of such nonsense I ran out of voice and, fortunately, the CBC was out of film. But not before they had captured the highlights of my lecture and many beautiful expressions on faces registering shock, scorn, humor and confusion.

As a result of the Sunday performance in Hyde Park, an invitation was extended by the BBC for me to appear on their top-rated nightly news show, *24 Hours,* conducted by Charles Michaelmore. Jeanne was particularly impressed because she had noticed Michaelmore's figure in wax at Madame Tussard's famous museum—one of the few living personalities to be so immortalized.

The taping session was set for the following Wednesday

evening at Shepherd's Bush Studio. Late that afternoon an attractive young lady showed up at our hotel door with a male escort and she interviewed me for BBC radio. Finished in half an hour, the man and woman offered to drive me to the studio. I begged off—the taping was still two hours away—to relax and make some final preparations. They were most persistant, saying they would wait in the lobby. Again I refused.

Jeanne was a little annoyed by their steadfast desire to take care of me. I was amused by such overt hospitality; nevertheless, she felt I should keep my radar in good working order for whatever lay ahead.

I arrived at the BBC studio on time and was greeted by Mr. Michaelmore's valet. He offered me a drink in a small room off the foyer. Reluctant to explain that I don't drink, I excused myself with the next best truth: "I never drink after dinner."

There were still ten minutes before the taping and I was led upstairs to another room—the "client's booth." And this time there was a drink waiting for me already poured. How considerate! And how odd. In America an actor could be suspended for drinking on the job. I waved it away with another explanation: "I never drink before an interview."

The valet and a studio aide shrugged, exchanged glances (here was an apparent square?) and led me into the main studio. The cameras were already warmed up, technicians in position and floodlights on full. My interviewer was a kindly old gentleman who seemed to be in his late seventies. He sat waiting for me in one of two director's chairs that faced each other. Before we could be introduced a voice boomed over the P.A. system, "Quiet now, tape rolling, ten, nine, eight, seven. . . ."

What efficiency and timing, I thought to myself. It was exactly 8:00 P.M. and I barely made it to my chair before the interviewer began with his first question:

"Mr. Abel, I understand that your campaign to clothe all animals was interwith on the decided and shocked insense. Is that true?"

As we had just returned from Scotland where I couldn't understand the English language at all, I immediately assumed this man was a Scot. In order not to embarrass him, I answered as though I understood the question.

"You could say that, sir. Furthermore, our organization is known around the world and some of our most influential supporters are English."

"Well," he continued soberly, "that may be true, but I ask you if S.I.N.A. with all its conversomes could manage to suffern without comfort."

The poor fellow must be senile, I thought, as he mumbled away words, speaking gibberish. Surely the BBC would not allow such an unintelligible interviewer unless— Suddenly it dawned on me. I was facing a master double-talk artist! There was only one way to cope: answer every question intelligently, no matter what he asked.

Back and forth we went. He with some of the finest double-talk ever heard on the British tube. I never faltered, answering every question with a straight answer. (Only much later that evening was I to learn that he was one of England's best, Sir Stanley Unwin.)

From time to time, out of the corner of my eye, I could detect the cameramen holding their sides, desperately trying not to laugh out loud at the comedy such deadpan partners provoked.

Unwin never once broke character as he battered away

at me: "But Mr. Abel, you have been quoted in the States as saying that animals have no sense of sin, that the whole world is their bedroom. Now would you consider this ansin on morals a resolution?"

That girl! Those drinks! No preshow conversation with my interviewer—all part of an elaborate plot to put me on!

"No," I answered after deliberating for several seconds. "We as humans go around censoring statues by putting fig leaves on them out of a sense of personal guilt over our own sexual embarrassment."

"You made your point very well there. Are you convinced that television interviewers are so incredibly gullible?"

This was Unwin's only straight question, obviously meant to dramatize the situation he thought I didn't know I was in. I played along with him.

"I think they are a little too smug at times, perhaps brainwashed by their own sense of invincibility. A serious demeanor shouldn't necessarily imply a serious intent. For example, my latest campaign concerns the growth of the big toe. I suspect it is leaping forth at the horrendous rate of $1/100$ of an inch a year! Did you know that?"

"No, I didn't," stammered Unwin, suddenly aware I had turned the tables and was interviewing him.

"Well, you should be concerned about it," I said playfully as Michaelmore signaled Unwin to end the interview.

"Yes, I'll do a deep jerring on it," he promised. "And thank you very much, Mr. Abel, for underlining the human behind."

It was all over in half an hour. The studio lights dimmed, Sir Stanley Unwin gave me a crisp good-by handshake and disappeared out the door. I was alone with

Michaelmore and he had a quizzical look on his face. Did I know what had transpired? Was it a success or a failure? I played the innocent dupe, thanked him for the opportunity to appear on *24 Hours* and took a taxi back to my hotel.

I wanted Michaelmore and Unwin to believe I had been their patsy. Otherwise they would have scrapped the interview and never put it on the air. I had learned this from past experience when Jeanne, posing as Mrs. Yetta Bronstein, had so unnerved an interviewer that the video tape wasn't aired.

Promptly at 10:30 P.M. the show went on the air as Jeanne and I watched the set in our room with anticipation. Michaelmore opened with a few introductory remarks that explained my past track record for successfully hoaxing Americans. Then he proclaimed a victory for the BBC and England, boasting that he had trapped me into being interviewed by Sir Stanley Unwin without my knowing what was happening! That I had been taken. The tape was played exactly as recorded and Michaelmore spoke smugly at the conclusion:

"I wonder if Mr. Abel still believes that we're all such a gullible lot as he watches from his hotel room. After we recorded that interview Mr. Abel gave no sign at all that there was anything odd about the questions. He left our studios happily talking about his voyage back to America tomorrow."

For the first time in my life I had a vague notion what it felt like to be tarred and feathered. Jeanne was so miffed by Michaelmore she wanted to rush right over to Madame Tussaud's Museum and put a match to his effigy.

When we arrived at Southampton the next morning for our trip back to the states aboard the *Queen Elizabeth,* we found ourselves the objects of unexpected attention. Apparently all of England watches 24 *Hours* with a kind of religious fervor and my sparring match with Unwin had topped anything ever seen for sheer comic delight.

"Great show!" shouted a porter as he ran to grab our bags.

"Never saw anything like it," said the man at the currency exchange desk.

"You and old Stanley really went at it!" laughed one of the boarding personnel.

We were whisked through customs with smiles and congratulations on all sides from the usually grim officials who handled such formalities.

A public relations man for the Cunard Lines met us in our cabin and requested that we follow him to meet the press. When Jeanne and I entered a suite on the promenade deck it was filled with reporters and we found ourselves in the middle of a question and answer session:

"Did Stanley Unwin know that you knew, or did you know?"

"What are the people like in Britain, compared to the States?"

"Do you have a really big hoax planned you can tell us about?"

I couldn't imagine why the press was assembled for us, and they weren't. Actress Hayley Mills and film producer Roy Boulting were expected any minute. We were just kind of standing in for them to keep the reporters busy.

We had hoped for a quiet five-day ride home aboard that lovely ship. No such luck. Both Jeanne and I were asked to lecture the passengers on our adventures, which we did. We attended numerous cocktail parties, including a special one with the ship's captain. And everybody, passengers and crew, plied us with questions wherever we went.

I was responsible for only one hoax during the trip. In the dining room, two days out to sea, I whispered confidentially to our waiter that the *Queen* was being tracked by an Egyptian submarine flying a white sheet on her periscope. The next day passengers peered out over the waters trying vainly to sight the sub. One man had a telescope, others used binoculars.

Finally, after the wild rumor spread all the way down into the engine room, one of the ship's officers announced that no conventional submarine—even if Egypt had one—could ever match the *Queen Elizabeth*'s top speed. As proof, he cited her World War II record for transporting troops to Europe without a convoy.

SIXTEEN

A.T.&T.
(ACTIVATED TOES
AND TRAINING)

Whenever I felt the need to test a satirical concept, I generally headed for one of the radio talk shows, or better yet, the Alan Burke TV show. Burke's show was taped before an audience of some size and he encouraged "unusual" people to come forward at the beginning of each program and state their beef, or whatever.

One of my monologues was on the growth of the big toe. I had already written an essay on this crazy theme for the San Francisco *Chronicle* that produced some lively reactions. Now I wanted to test it as a "put on" with Alan Burke as my target.

So I made my way over to WNEW-TV on East Sixty-seventh Street in New York one Thursday evening in the spring of 1967 and asked the uniformed guard for the producer. He sent around an associate producer, Michael

Shapiro, who was intrigued with my campaign and suggested I go to the head of the line.

"You'll be on first, Mr. Spencer," he said, eyeing me suspiciously. I was dressed in an ordinary business suit and looked normal enough, but I suspected Shapiro read me as a real loon. "And when I give you the signal, go up to the podium microphone and tell Mr. Burke about your campaign," he added.

Shapiro led me into the studio past a line of several hundred people waiting to get in. They were of all ages and not unlike any normal group lined up to see the freak show at Palisades Amusement Park. One chap had a slice of pizza in his hand; others chewed popcorn or munched on potato chips. Some carried sandwiches and small thermos jugs. Everybody seemed to be in a jolly mood, but I had an uneasy feeling that the crowds waiting to see the Christians thrown to the lions acted the same way!

I was given a seat near the mike and the audience soon filled up every available space on the risers. Producer Paul Nobel made a short speech warning us not to smoke, not to leave our seats for any reason and not to eat when Burke was speaking.

The house lights went down and the floodlights came on. Nobel led the audience in sustained applause for Burke's entrance and I was motioned to stand up before the mike. After a few commercials and comments from Burke, he looked toward me and asked that I state my name and purpose:

"Mr. Burke," I began. "My name is Bruce Spencer and I am President of the New York Chapter of A.T.&T. That's Activated Toes and Training."

The audience laughed and Burke shook his head in disbelief as I continued: "I am here to enlist your support in a problem that is even greater than Communists or air pollution. It concerns the growth of the big toe, which is leaping forth at the horrendous rate of 1/100 of an inch a year. I discovered this alarming fact when I was making a study of the recession of the little toe. It was to my horror I learned that as the little toe recedes into the foot, it's pushing the big toe out! I would like to measure your big toe and prove to you without a shadow of a doubt that you could be suffering from what I call extended toe-itus. Now many people here in the audience seem to be amused. But I challenge them to look at their own toes tonight and then measure them three months from now. They would find that the big toe is leaping forth without restraint. Why, within a matter of twenty years we're all going to have giant toes that will burst right through our shoes!"

Along with the laughter there were hisses and boos. Several red-faced men wearing white side-walled haircuts with matching socks glared at me sternly. I forged ahead:

"Shoe manufacturers know this but they aren't talking. They just make pointy-toed shoes. Why do you think they make open-toed shoes for women? So the big toe can sneak out and breathe. If we don't take positive action and arrest the growth of the big toe now, people are going to lose their balance, turn to alcohol, sex and other sins. I have here documented proof going back to the fourteenth century by the noted Professor Sweinberger who first noticed his daughter Clara's big toe slipping out. He discovered this was responsible for her being backward. And she became a very unfortunate child who went to live in the trees with the animals. Which is where we may all find ourselves. With your permission, Mr. Burke, I would be very happy to measure your big toe. . . ."

"I allow no one to touch my body," said Burke facetiously.

"I'm not interested in your body, Mr. Burke, except in the name of science. If there is anyone in the audience who would like to participate in this experiment . . . this gentleman over here looks good," I said and pointed to a man weighing around 250 pounds.

My victim was a good enough sport. He sat on the stage floor and removed his shoes and socks as Burke held his nose and pretended nausea. I took out a caliper, measured the man's big toe and sprayed his feet with Dr. Scholl's foot deodorant while maintaining a running commentary:

". . . I teach biology part time, Mr. Burke, at Americana College in Mineral City, Ohio. I also sell shoes on the side . . . to make ends meet. This man has a big toe that measures at this time point oh, oh, six seven. That's a little smaller than the average male's . . . toe. Now if you will remember that figure, sir, and look me up in about three months, I'll take another reading. And keep in mind that Toenology is important to your peace of mind."

In response to shouts from the audience to explain Toenology I told them that "Toenology is to the toe as phrenology is to the head and astology is to another part of the body. For example, in Toenology, if you stub your toe against furniture you're clumsy. If you walk pigeon-toed, you don't know which way you're going. A person who tippy-toes on the street to avoid dog residue is cautious. And the man who walks on his heels in public is practically always a coward."

I left the studio during the commercial and as I made my way through the audience every face was examining mine. My attitude was somber. Their expressions did not reflect disbelief—although they had laughed uproariously —but, rather a morbid curiosity. Just for fun I twitched my left cheek at a teen-age girl who stared at me wide-eyed. Frightened, she grabbed her girl friend's hand for safety.

Flushed with the success of my "big toe" routine on *The Alan Burke Show,* I decided to try for more television exposure. This time my target was Art Stark, producer of the ABC-TV afternoon program *Wedding Party.* A few years back, when Stark was producing Johnny Carson's *Tonight Show,* he had auditioned me and then decided too many people would recognize me if I did any kind of put-on with Carson. I wanted to prove to my own satisfaction that he himself wouldn't recognize me, let alone the public.

Wedding Party advertised in newspapers for unusual couples and I promptly mailed some A.T.&T. literature to Stark's office.

A few days later both Jeanne and I were called in for an interview. Stark showed no signs of recognizing me.

The next day I received a call from Stark's chief writer, Woody Kling, who asked:

"What do you call the big toe in medical terms?"

"Well, I'm not familiar with the technical terms, Mr. Kling, because this experiment of mine is only for lay people; I'm not a doctor or an anthropologist, just a researcher."

"Well, do larger people tend to have larger toes and smaller people smaller toes?"

"I would say yes, more or less, but mostly no. Let me say this. The length of the big toe can be related to one's height and width, but its tendency to grow is perhaps based upon diet, air pollution and physical activity involving the foot—particularly in humid climates."

"O.K. We'll be in touch."

Two weeks later Jeanne and I were on the show as "toe tutors." I claimed that I first met my wife when I researched the growth of two thousand big toes—and naturally I fell in love with my wife's big toe at first sight.

Al Hamil, the M.C., seemed delighted to have such a kooky team spark the program with our crazy antics. I measured his big toe and rattled off nonsense figures to Jeanne, who took notes. Then I sprayed his foot "to prevent any loose germs from attacking the audience."

"How does it look?" asked Hamil.

"You have a very nice toe," I replied soberly.

"But does it always tickle like this?"

"Yes. That's one of my main problems in my research. Some people get hysterical with laughter. It's very disturbing to me."

Before, during and after the show I passed Art Stark numerous times, but he still didn't recognize me, although we nodded and said hello to one another. One of his assistants, a girl named Vicki, asked what the foot spray was.

"It's right out of my own lab, a mixture called FU-2," I explained. "FU-1 caused a fungus that could be carried from foot to foot—we called it 'toe main poisoning'—but my new and improved formula prevents it."

Vicki mentioned that she formerly held a job with the

Cornell Medical School, doing research on various viruses, and how boring it all was.

"I suppose looking at toes all day long can get pretty tiring, too," she ventured.

"Yes," I sighed. "It does get you down after a while."

She also wondered how 1/100 of an inch a year in growth could result in four or five inches after only a few years.

"I suspect drinking has a lot to do with it, but I'm not sure," I replied.

"Is this growth an individual one or based upon evolution?" she asked.

This girl was asking me questions more provocative than the ones on the show! "It's much too early to make any definitive statements at this time," I replied slowly. "But I hope people wake up before an advanced stage of elongitus toe-itis sets in."

She nodded understandingly and left.

For our participation on the show Jeanne and I received a stereo record player, a week's vacation in Grand Bahama and five cases of peanut butter. Not a bad reward for a bit of nonsense and to prove my point that I am seldom if ever recognized. Even people I know sometimes don't say hello to me.

SEVENTEEN

THE NIGHT NBC
WENT OFF THE AIR

Long John Nebel is one of the most outspoken and feared radio personalities in New York City. His nightly program is beamed out from NBC on fifty thousand watts and reaches people in as many as thirty states, judging by the postmarks on his hate mail.

For at least ten years I had tried unsuccessfully to get booked on his show. I enjoyed Long John's intense manner, his irascible humor and vitriolic comments that unsettled many a guest. To me his show was a sort of hardnosed fantasy—Nebel, as the Giant with the Golden Goose, determined to squash any Jack who climbed up his bean stalk. I thought it would be fun to spar with him a little.

So when his secretary, Roberta Kopper, called one June afternoon and invited me to debate Long John

Nebel, I was delighted. She mentioned I was scheduled for the Friday night before the Fourth of July weekend. Millions of vacationers would be on the highways, their car radios turned on to distract them from a long drive and the hot weather. NBC Radio would likely have its largest tune-in audience of the year.

I arrived at the National Broadcasting Company, 30 Rockefeller Plaza, around 7:45 P.M., made my way through the lines of tourists and signed an autograph for a woman who thought I was Alan King. She handed me a program to *Fiddler on the Roof* and I obligingly wrote "To Debbie with love, Alan" on the cover. Then I proceeded to the fifth floor as I had been instructed. Opposite the bank of elevators on that floor were two glass-windowed studios. Long John was already on the air in one of them with a fifteen-minute talk show that preceeded his 8 to 9 P.M. "Versus" show.

As Long John shouted angrily at some woman caller for being stupid I went to the rear of his studio, where the control room was located. Nebel's producer was there with an engineer. He motioned for me to wait out in the hall.

I returned to the hall and spent the next ten minutes pacing outside the elevators. There was no place to sit so I watched the elevators go up and down.

Five minutes before air time I was ushered into Long John's studio by a woman who said flatly, "This way, please." She pointed out a chair at a small table opposite which Nebel sat. He was reading a copy of *Newsweek* and didn't look up. I cleared my throat. Nebel turned a page and continued reading, as though he were completely oblivious of my presence. Somewhat meekly I said, "Nice day." There was absolute silence.

Still without looking up, Nebel buzzed the woman who had escorted me in. When she stuck her head through the studio door he mumbled "Coffee." I was about to add, "Me, too, for my parched throat," but thought it best not to. There was something strained going on between Long John Nebel and me. I had better cool it until I knew just what was up.

Almost absentmindedly Nebel reached into his pocket and took out a pack of king-sized cigarettes. He took one cigarette, lit it, placed the package just out of my reach and continued reading without looking up.

I thought to myself, even a captured Viet Cong gets at least a cigarette and a drink of water! I wondered if this harsh and crude treatment was part of Nebel's psychological attempt to irritate me sufficiently so I would perform more antagonistically. Well, if he was telling he how to behave, I was certainly going to pull out all the stops.

We had about thirty seconds before airtime when the girl brought in Nebel's coffee and, thoughtfully, a glass of water for him. Both of these items were placed carefully beyond my reach. Then the red light flashed above the control room and we were on the air. Still without looking at me, Nebel spoke directly into his mike through clenched teeth:

"Mr. Abel, you claim that you hoaxed the American public. You admit that you deceived the press and the public. And I was wondering if you can think of one good reason why anyone should be interested in doing business with you on any level when you admit that you've been a charlatan!"

"If you have children," I replied coldly, "which I doubt now that you've talked a little bit, I would say that you've told them about Santa Claus. And since Santa Claus is a fairytale, then *you'd* be a charlatan."

Nebel quickly denied he had ever told his children there was a Santa Claus.

"Then you're an unkind man!" I countered. "Because anyone who denies a child the right to have a Santa Claus is a cruel man."

Nebel argued lamely that he wanted to be a cruel man. I interrupted him: "You're only agreeing with me because you have no other answer," I replied forcefully. "Now I've written a book. You haven't read the book, obviously, because you're not talking intelligently. . . ."

I was drawing blood. Nebel asked heatedly how I could determine whether he talked intelligently.

"Well," I said slowly. "I can only judge by looking at you and hearing you. I have nothing else to go by. Do you have one of your I.Q. tests handy? Did you get a dis— an honorable discharge from the army? I'm sorry I said 'dishonorable' . . . I didn't mean that. . . ."

Nebel angrily warned me that this was going to be one of the unhappiest nights I had ever spent.

"Fine," I snapped back, "because I've met your friend, Joe Pyne, on the Coast and he's in love with himself. The same as you are, I'm sure. . . ."

"Have you ever made a success of anything except making a damn fool of yourself?" shouted Nebel. "Which you are now!"

"I admit that I enjoy making a fool out of myself," I said calmly. "But you can't because you aren't big enough. You have to have little people and bigots that you can chew up because it makes you feel large. You see, Hitler did the same thing. He hired a man called Goebbels. . . ."

At this point Nebel and I engaged in a rhubarb, each of us talking over the other. The effect must have been quite shocking to listeners; only occasionally could words be understood.

When the smoke cleared a bit I started off in another direction:

"You might mention my book, *The Great American Hoax,* and the publisher, Trident Press, because you've already plugged your own book for the last fifteen minutes, John, and it's been out of print for years. You shouldn't *do* that without mentioning *my* book too."

Nebel turned pale, practically bit the top of his mike off and called me a *fink*.

"I've been called worse names," I admitted casually. "It does take one to know one. And I can laugh at myself. But you can't laugh at yourself when you are known as a . . . well, I'll call you a crumb, because I don't like to call people finks. A fink is an all-purpose term. A crumb is also a person who goes on the air and uses little people to provide entertainment for. . . ."

Nebel became livid with rage. He pounded the table and launched into his own tirade against me. I paid no attention to him. Whenever there was an opening, even the slightest pause, I jumped in:

"I can interrupt you as much as you interrupt me . . . you're a ridiculous guy! Look, Randi—oops, I'm sorry, Long John, whatever your name is. Let's try to get some meaningful discussion going here. You want to talk, hold up your hand and I'll let you talk . . . look, we don't have much time. . . . People are listening in their cars, probably running off the road now trying to understand this crazy conversation. It's a very dangerous night to drive, so let's try to make some sense. Also, I think people are tired of your voice. You're on the air every night. Why don't you give me a chance to talk a little bit?"

Nebel shouted that he would never plug my book and he accused me of being a puzzle.

"We ought to talk about *The Great American Hoax* in nice terms for a while and then we can chew each other up a little bit, and do a Joe Pyne act . . ." I replied sharply.

I was surprised that Nebel didn't retain his cool and his anger seemed quite genuine to me. He was making frantic signals toward the control to have my mike turned off. They didn't do it. I kept right on:

"*The Great American Hoax* was merely a spoof. It was something to have fun with. . . . John, we can fight a little later. O.K.? Fine. Thank you. My book is a compilation of four or five years of idiocy, of nonsense. . . ."

"*Just a moment,*" said Nebel as he waved wildly and knocked his package of cigarettes on to the floor.

"Now *you* wait a minute!" I admonished him sharply, shaking my finger in his face. "People don't even know what we're talking about. You haven't established what this interview is all about. You care only what *you* think. And that's not important right now. Because we're here to talk about a very important book, *The Great American Hoax,* published by Trident Press, $4.95 at your local bookstore. . . ."

Underneath my "commercial" Long John Nebel maintained a running attack against me. His voice kept getting higher, almost near the soprano range. He ordered me to stop talking and get out of the studio.

"No, *I'm* not going to leave," I said determinedly, "although I hear that all your guests walk out on you. Why don't I place you under a citizen's arrest? Because if you act this way you're an obscene person and you must violate some law. Is there an officer on the grounds? Any patrol cars not answering a call? Come on up here, fellas, I want to give you Long John. . . ."

"*All right, you've had it! You're through!*" screamed Nebel.

"Come on, John," I pleaded. "Why don't you talk to me until nine o'clock? Why not pretend to be a nice person?"

At this point Nebel looked towards the control room and cut his throat with his finger, a signal to his producer to take the show off the air. NBC Radio suddenly went to music as Long John and I sat and glared at each other. Both his hands were tightly clenched and his face was white as a sheet.

As soothing organ music flowed out over the fifty thousand watts of New York's most powerful radio station, the NBC switchboard was lit up like a Christmas tree. Thousands of stunned listeners called in to find out who strangled whom. Also, startled station officials poured into our studio from elevators, washrooms and offices. We were soon surrounded by thirty or forty people milling about, whispering in hushed tones:

"What happened?"

"It sounded like a real fight."

"Is Long John really upset?"

"Who is this guy with him?"

"Never saw him before."

"Long John never blows up."

"This is a first for him—I heard every word!"

Long John and I remained seated. Suddenly he shouted

at me, "You ruined my show! Get the hell out of here!"

"I will *not* leave, John," I said determinedly. "You invited me to be your guest here for a full hour and we still have forty minutes to go. You want to play games, fine. But I will not leave now and permit you to do a hatchet job on me when I can't defend myself. I'm staying right here."

Now the music was quietly changed to the lush strings of David Rose and this gave the interrupted program a more pronounced feeling of restful calm. But it was forced and the listening audience had to know something was wrong. The calls into NBC mounted in intensity.

Jeanne was at home listening and her first thought was one of technical difficulty in transmission. But as the music went on and on with no explanation she suspected a studio rhubarb and tried to call me through the NBC switchboard. Every single line was busy.

Nebel looked right through me when he spoke again, as though in a trance: "I want you to leave right now and that's that!"

I shook my head and sat there. He gave some more secret hand signals to his producer, who had two phones going now in the control room, one cradled on each shoulder. His hands were busy pushing the eighteen or twenty line buttons on a white telephone call director. More people herded into the studio. It was becoming unbearably hot and smoke filled the room.

Bearded Brad Crandall, who followed Nebel's program with a talk show of his own, had a slight smile on his face. The entire scene was Kafkaesque. I could hardly believe all this was happening in one of the nation's largest and more conservative radio stations.

To add to the bizarre situation a large group of tourists

stood outside the studio window, their noses pressed against the glass, watching intently. Their guide was desperately trying to move them on to the next stop. They refused to budge. Something exciting was happening here and they wanted to be where the action was.

When two NBC security guards entered the studio with more station personnel, some of the tourists sneaked in, too. The studio was now jam-packed with people. I kept my hand on my wallet. Nebel still sat gazing at me, taking long, deep drags on his cigarette, now down to a quarter-inch butt.

"John," I said lightly. "Why don't you go home and let me finish the program alone. I won't say anything nasty about you."

Nebel didn't say a word. He just continued glaring. So I made myself comfortable and picked up his *Newsweek* magazine. Now it was my time to read and ignore him.

We had already been off the air about ten muintes. Ray Conniff and his chorus and orchestra were playing "June Is Bustin' Out All Over" when the two burly uniformed guards took up a position directly behind me. Conversations tapered off and stopped.

"Gentlemen," I said in a loud voice. "I am a nonviolent performer who will go limp at the base of this microphone if anyone attempts to remove me from this studio until the show is over. Furthermore, if anyone were to bruise my skin, I can guarantee you I'll break out in an incurable skin rash. It might cost NBC fifty thousand dollars in health fees for my recovery."

The two guards shuffled away to a neutral corner and waited for new orders. There were more frantic meetings and discussions in the control room. Long John went inside and engaged in some animated arguments with his

producer and several men who seemed to be NBC executives. Finally Nebel came out and whispered something to the guards. They moved back into position
directly behind me.

Nebel's secretary came running out of the control room
and told him that reporters from *The New York Times,*
the *Daily News* and the *New York Post* were all on the
phones demanding a statement. He waved her aside with
a brusk "Don't tell them anything." Somebody started to
clear the studio and we were back on the air with our
"interview."

The final portion of the program was about as dull,
listless and uninspired a conversation as ever was heard on
radio. No reference was made to the battle, no attempt
was made to explain its sudden cutoff from the air. Nebel
asked me stock questions about my activities as a hoaxer
and I answered him with stock replies. Nebel hardly
looked at me when he spoke and I reciprocated by pretending to be more interested in *Newsweek* magazine. I
was, however, very conscious of the uniformed and armed
guards within striking distance.

Afterwards, Nebel, his producer and secretary—clutching a tape of the show—were whisked out of the studio
to a waiting elevator. Escorted by the two guards, they
all disappeared down the shaft. And I was left all alone.
Through the control-room window I could see white lights
flashing on the call director and private phones. But
there wasn't a soul there to answer. Everybody had vanished.

The *New York Post* television and radio critic, Bob
Williams, planned a Page One story for the next day, but
his editor vetoed the position as too sensational. Williams

then devoted his regular "On the Air" column to the fracas, saying in part:

> An exasperated Long John Nebel, a veteran practitioner of talk-show controversy, cut his WNBC Radio program off the air and played music last night after a name-calling brawl with public hoaxer Alan Abel got out of hand. Long John's faithful followers bombarded WNBC with phone calls when recorded music replaced his nightly "Versus" show. . . .

Williams went on to quote our verbal exchanges and ended with the comment, "After nine minutes of negotiation, the music stopped and the two resumed a peaceful but comparatively dull discussion of Abel's exploits."

When Nebel's girl Friday, Roberta Kopper, left him for *The Alan Burke Show*, she told me that the entire broadcasting industry around New York was "chuckling with great glee" for weeks after the blow-up. And I heard from unofficial sources that underground tapes of the air battle were selling like hotcakes.

As a postscript, in all fairness to Long John Nebel, he turned out to be one of the few broadcasters who can take it as well as dish it out. I was invited back a few months later for an all-night show with him, and Jeanne appeared on a subsequent program as Yetta Bronstein.

EIGHTEEN

THE FIRST TOPLESS
STRING QUARTET

Historians will undoubtedly note of us that in our time
we conquered and cured most diseases, explored the
moon and also discovered nudity. It took thousands of
years of evolution for man to come by the double-breasted
suit. Yet in spite of this accomplishment and others, today's man is more fascinated by a surreptitious glimpse
of his fellow in his aboriginal state.

This wave of nudity began sweeping the country in
1965, starting in San Francisco, when bare-bosomed wait-
resses won out over the voice of public outrage—small as
it was—for the right to expose double-breasted bosoms.
The debate of the City Fathers over the question of "to
pastie or not to pastie" was pretty ludicrous, but no more
so than the view my wife and I had when we visited a
topless restaurant in San Francisco. Jeanne ordered the

Avocado Surprise and I had the Chicken Salad Delight. The great moment came when our waitress delivered the order, two huge bowls of salad, and she stood at our table trying to decide who ordered which.

Along with the topless craze, once amateur-quality nudist magazines became bolder and slicker. A dance troupe from California performed a ballet at Hunter College during which the dancers, both male and female, took off all their clothes. To top them, the Living Theatre encouraged the audience to take off *their* clothes! And many did.

The long arm of the law disrupted the concert of cellist Charlotte Moorman when she removed two battery operated propellers from her whirling breasts and played the "Opera Sextronomique" topless. If the police hadn't panicked at that moment—and at least waited until the climax of the performance—they could have pinched a completely nude cellist.

A criminal court justice gave Miss Moorman a suspended sentence for what he called an "immature and lewd performance." Then the judge went on to make comment in his own defense: "There are those who might shout that I am a square and stagnant in my thinking and that I do not understand the new dimensions in art. This noise emanates from a mighty vocal minority."

But it takes more than a minority to make a smashing success on Broadway. Such a show was the musical entitled *Hair*, which broke the genital barrier by featuring open nudity, both sexes. For the first time since the hippie movement began, it became possible to distinguish the girls from the boys.

While the world wondered how long it would be before the ultimate act would be performed on stage, I felt it was time for me to make a comment on the national nudity scene. To me, nudity as a fad was amusing. And to pay the high price of a theater ticket for a view of what you could see in your own full-length mirror for free was ridiculous. So I found myself composing the following press release which I sent out to a few newspapers for their reactions:

FOR IMMEDIATE RELEASE

THE FIRST TOPLESS STRING QUARTET will be France's first gift to America since the Statue of Liberty. These four qualified musicians have played to sitting room only audiences on the continent and will soon be in America to show off their titular talents.

By performing topless the girls have been able to produce an unhampered series of tones that leave the audience breathless. Thousands of people who once hated chamber music now love it. As one renowned music critic wrote: "Not even the Juilliard String Quartet could have better box office appeal in the nude than these girls have."

Although none of the members of THE FIRST TOPLESS STRING QUARTET are married, they do not believe in nudity per se. Nor are they exhibitionists or "kooks." They are just dedicated to the survival of live music and feel that by disrobing they can make their point—using nudity as a common denominator of interest to eliminate the barriers that exist between classical and popular music lovers.

The quartet hopes to record an album with a major company while in the States, but they will continue to perform only for private concerts under strict conformity to local laws. Their manager intends to avoid embarrassing situations that might lead to the violation of prurient community standards and further strain existing relationships between France and the United States.

Meantime, public reaction to THE FIRST TOPLESS STRING QUARTET can best be summed up through the words of a prominent law enforcement official who said: "These girls represent the only nude attraction I ever seen outside the court that has socially redeeming values."

The following day there was a phone call for me from Jean Crafton, a reporter with the New York *Post*. She wanted more information. I happened to be looking at my daily reminder and saw the notation to call Jack Gold. So on the spot I made up the name "Jacques Goldetsky" as conductor of the quartet. When she pressed for a specific concert date, I compulsively ad-libbed a date a few weeks hence. But, feigning concern that the group's concerts must remain private—to avoid embarrassing the girls by a police raid—I declined to say where. Therefore she had no way of checking.

Miss Crafton also wanted the girls' names, so I boldly borrowed them from a Paris street map I had been studying—Madeleine, Boucher, Tronchet.

The next day in the *Post* there appeared a straight story headlined "Bach, Beethoven, Brahms and Bosoms" * that said:

Although Mayor Lindsay and Governor Rockefeller banned it in restaurants, toplessness in the concert hall is on its way to Fun City. A group billed as the FIRST TOPLESS STRING QUARTET, composed of four Bach-playing bosomy French women, has scheduled a concert here June 18th. They plan to give their 90-minute performance naked from the waist up. Under the direction of pianist Jacques Goldetsky, also topless, the group has played Europe for the past two years and has scheduled summer concerts in Philadelphia, Cleveland, Chicago, Denver, Seattle, San Diego, San Francisco and Los Angeles, in addition to their New York appearance.

The quartet avoids clashes with local authorities because all concerts are private, with tickets being sold by invitation only. The in-group, mostly the Jet Set, buy the tickets, their

* Reprinted by permission of New York Post. © 1967, New York Post Corporation.

manager said, adding that "the people involved are highly educated, obviously not blue noses."

But he refused to disclose where the New York concert will be held, saying he feared some "prudes" in the city might try to get the engagement canceled if they knew where it was.

Members of the group include: first violinist Michele Andre, second violinist Gretchen Gansebrust, cellist Madeleine Boucher and violist Maria Tronchet. Miss Andre said she preferred to play breasts bared "because garments hinder my movements. I can bow more freely and feel closer to Bach, my favorite, when I play partially undressed."

It's uncertain what the Old Master and church organist would say to that!

More phone calls and telegrams came in as a result of this initial publicity by the *Post* with its half-million circulation. Joy Miller of the Associated Press took a story over the phone and asked for photographs. To her reportorial credit, she exercised some skepticism. "It's either a very elaborate and entertaining hoax or it really exists, I don't know," she said, waiting for me to inform her by either protest or surrender. But I never would confess to someone who had to ask. Besides, the newspapers are so full of murder and war casualties and all other possible ugliness and misery, people need a laugh, a pleasant shocker, a comment on the absurdities in life. There *should* be a topless string quartet.

Ronald E. Cohen from United Press International contacted me for an interview with the girls. And others wanted tickets for the upcoming concert. Jeffry Barron of National Features Syndicate wired from Chicago for pictures. Viggo Steenstrup, who represented newspapers in Sweden and Denmark, wanted pictures. What could I do now? I promised them pictures "as soon as the negatives arrived from Europe."

Obviously I wasn't about to produce a real topless string quartet. Although Heaven knows it would be a tremendous commercial success overnight! While I entertained the idea briefly, I knew it would be impossible to find four serious violinists who would be willing to play in the raw. And just as difficult to find four nudists who could fiddle. Besides, my wife wouldn't let me. She reminded me that my interest lay in satirizing the nudity movement with the *illusion* of concertizing in the nude.

Jeanne and I talked the situation over and we decided to fake some photographs and see how far the joke would go before being discovered. We agreed to allow a maximum of $250 for this topless project. So far, the expenses had been limited to $2 for one hundred press releases, $6 for postage and $2 for the envelopes, a total of $10. There were also Jeanne's services for typing, folding, licking stamps, stuffing and sealing envelopes. However, I was usually able to take this out in trade. I mean things like running the sweeper, emptying the garbage and taking the deposit bottles back to the store.

If a photograph would satisfy the reporters, then that was our objective—to take a photograph of a topless string quartet. We would hire four figure models to hold stringed instruments. I designed the entire campaign within our budget limitations and, to keep the press interested, sent out another release that quoted what some of the critics had to say about the quartet's music:

Beethoven's Quartet in E minor (Op. 59 #2) sounded both feminine and clear-eyed. The slow movement was hypnotic and the fast section demonstrated the sheer frenzy of their headlong momentum.
                    —OTTO KLEINHAUS (Hamburg, W. Germany)

While their sentimentality is sometimes sticky, they play with an abandon that warmed the cockles of my heart. Truly an important musical experience for me.

—Sven Havidz (Copenhagen, Denmark)

Schermerhorn's Shimmy, although a light work of nonsense, was performed with immediacy, poetry, and complete fulfillment. Bravo, bravo, bravo to four beautiful girls who must have spent a good many hours playing with Kreutzer!

—Pierre Montenard (Paris, France)

"The 1937 Sextet for String Quartet, Clarinet and Piano" by Aaron Copland, with Archie Woomser playing the reed part on his trumpet, was magnificent. Pianist Jacques Goldetsky was on top of the piano part and the ensemble joined in a fun performance . . . because that is the kind of music they play. There was a beautiful array of double stops and the melodies bubbled out like an act of nature.

—T.C.M. (Toronto, Canada)

It was an arresting display of talent. The audience howled with delight when they did the David Rose medley . . . backwards and forwards. Certaintly an *outstanding* group and they are at their finest with "Op Pop Art" music.

—Name Withheld by Request (Brussels, Belgium)

A reporter from *Life* wanted to know the names of the newspapers I quoted from, but I claimed I didn't know, that he could probably check on his own and find out. I was certain he wouldn't know where to begin looking. All these "reviews" I had compiled by taking bits and pieces from legitimate reviews in *The New York Times.* I was a little surprised that of the reporters and music critics who called me, after receiving this latest communique, none had caught on to one very glaring error which I'd inserted. This was the "1937 Sextet for String Quartet, Clarinet and Piano" by Aaron Copland—a legitimate piece of music—where I blatantly substituted a trumpet for the reed part, an unpardonable sin in classical music.

My next step was to advertise for figure models. I mailed an ad to the *Village Voice*, a weekly tabloid published in Greenwich Village that is noted for its outspoken attitudes, nude photos and four-letter words. I was astonished when they promptly rejected my ad, although it read simply:

WANTED
Four figure models, female, for commercial-type ad.
No experience necessary. Ages 21-45. $10 per hour.
Call Mrs. Jeanne Abel 4-6 P.M. at OX 7-5895.

According to Mrs. Fendrick at the *Village Voice*, they had been having some trouble with so-called figure model ads by photographers who were more interested in the girls than they were in their trade. I assured her our intentions were of the highest order, that the girls were to pose for a dignified chamber music photograph, topless, and that was all. I mentioned they would even be wearing formal skirts and gloves. But she wasn't willing to trust me over the phone.

I finally had to make a trip down to their office and personally convince the advertising manager to run my ad. He, too, was reluctant but finally agreed, after I paid in cash for the space. He warned me we had better be on the level.

I couldn't understand the *Voice*'s apprehension over my ad when I noticed some they were presently running: one chap wanted to hire girls who were "willing to be stared at"; another fellow offered "ballet lessons to businessmen only"; there was "social nudism at its best in the nearby Poconos"; a book called *The Exquisite Thing* that "opens a new frontier of sexual love"; a lecture entitled

"Multiple Loving—Is It Wrong?" And "courteous massages in the privacy of your own home." My favorite was an announcement that "a cockroach and a cat will be making it at the 13th Street Theatre this Saturday at 3 PM."

Out of curiosity Jeanne answered one of the ads in the *Village Voice* for "actresses who want to earn $100 a day in films." The producer wanted her to come over and audition—after 9 P.M. that evening—and he refused to supply any information about the kind of movies he was making—past, present or future.

Jeanne didn't follow up on his offer to audition, but a young and adventurous friend of ours decided she would. Laura called for an interview and was also told to come over that evening. She went to the address, a loft in a four-story walk-up, and found the film producer amidst piles of old newspapers, battered furniture and faded still photos from the first soundies out of Hollywood.

He was a man in his sixties and friendly enough. There was a pay phone on his wall that rang constantly. He always told callers they had the wrong number. After looking Laura over a bit he said he would like to add her to his file. Since she didn't have any photos he said they would make some immediately. Laura took off her hat and fluffed her hair. But he advised her to put it back on again; they were going out.

Down they went into a nearby subway station and he placed her inside one of those twenty-five cent automatic photo machines! Laura sat for the four prints, which she paid for because the producer didn't have the correct change, and he kept two of them. She decided not to return to his office for the "live audition" and took the subway home as long as it was so convenient.

The day my ad appeared in the *Village Voice* there were nearly a hundred calls. Jeanne and I scheduled as many as we could for Friday and the remaining ones over the following Monday and Tuesday. We were looking for four assorted types who, when seated together with stringed instruments, would resemble a realistic string ensemble. With sensitive faces and graceful hands. As far as the bosoms were concerned, we wanted one or two flat-chested models—a little calculated disappointment for Peeping Toms. And a courtesy to those more interested in music than girls. But most of the girls who responded were excessively endowed.

We saw all types. That is, we didn't *see* them undressed, we just interviewed. Beatniks and even matronly ones. A woman about fifty-five explained the difficulty she had in persuading her husband to allow her to answer our ad. "For years I've wanted to model corsets, and he would never let me," she sighed. (The woman thought we were a corset company that once had offices in the same building.)

So Jeanne explained, tactfully, the nature of the modeling job.

"Topless!" she shouted indignantly. "I thought this was for a corset ad! I would never consider posing topless. I thought it was bottomless!"

And she departed in a fluster of half-turns and double takes.

We settled on four girls, two of whom had some professional experience as figure models. The decision had been difficult to make. There were so many attractive ones, but beauty was not a prerequisite. We finally chose a tall, willowy, sophisticated type, an attractive French girl who had a country-fresh look, and a motherly type in her fifties. Also a nurse, a Negro, who was so friendly and game for new life experiences, we hired her even at the risk of being accused of Negro Tokenism, a current and insincere advertising practice. Finally, Larry Wolf, an actor who was completely bald, posed as the conductor, Jacques Goldetsky.

Our next problem was finding an auditorium we could rent for several hours of "rehearsal." I approached the rental agent at Carnegie's Recital Hall, but they wouldn't permit photographs of any nature to be taken on their stage. Judson Hall had too many doors to guard. We wanted to avoid being observed by some passing music lover who might panic and call the gendarmes. Steinway Hall was just perfect. It had a miniature stage complete with attractive drapes and an American flag. Along the walls, paintings and antique lamps offered a second backdrop. It was ideal for our purposes and supplied the perfect elegant drawing-room setting for chamber music.

We allowed two hours in which to photograph the girls. A guard was posted at the door and the only people allowed in, besides Jeanne and me and the girls, were photographer Maria Anastasio and Norman Forrest, a *bona fide* violist who was to coach the girls on how to hold their instruments properly.

During the session we played recordings of string quartet music to put the girls in a proper frame of mind—a serious one—because they were laughing at their ridiculous costumes: formal length skirts with cummerbunds that Jeanne had whipped up, elbow-length gloves, earrings, necklaces and, of course, nothing on top. The viola player was having a difficult time holding her instrument in position, because of her unusually large breasts. But coach Norman Forrest was right there to assist every time her bow drooped.

As things turned out we obtained some very striking photos that looked like a topless string quartet in the middle of a concert, rather than just a posed gag. I mailed out twenty photographs to various news sources and magazines, fairly certain that none of them would have the courage to print the photo. At least not without masking the exposed bosoms.

On May 15, 1967, *Life* magazine returned the photograph with a letter from George P. Hunt's editorial offices that said: "Thank you for sending the enclosed information about THE FIRST TOPLESS STRING QUARTET. That we are unable to publicize it, in no way lessens our appreciation of your thought. With best wishes. Sincerely yours, Ann Scott, for the Editors."

I sent one to *The Readers Digest*, curious for their response. They neither acknowledged it nor returned the photograph, quite unusual for that magazine with its reputation for being prompt and precise with rejections.

Look magazine rejected the proposed feature story with a letter from assistant editor Anne Celli: "The editors regret that they cannot consider an article on the Quartet as such a feature does not meet with *Look*'s editorial needs."

Quite surprising to me was the turn down from the *National Enquirer*—a standout in the areas of sex, sin and the sensational. Feature editor Bernard Scott wrote: "Sounds like a swinging idea but it didn't appeal to the man who matters here. I hope it goes well for you." It was an interesting rejection in view of their usual contents, baited with headlines like: "Virgin Cuts Up Lover"—

"Slave Girl Bites and Seduces Dog"—"98-Year-Old Man Rapes Teen-ager."

A personal letter arived from Mark Goodson, president of Goodson-Todman Productions:

> Thank you for your note about the Topless String Quar-
> tet. . . . I would like to know the following:
> 1. Where have they appeared?
> 2. What kind of music do they play?
> 3. Where can I see this outfit in person?
>
> Sincerely,
Mark Goodson

I didn't respond for a few days. Then came a hurry-up call from Jack O'Neil of the Goodson-Todman office, who asked me to send Jacques Goldetsky over for an interview. They wanted to consider him for *To Tell the Truth* and his secret would be simply that he conducted a topless string quartet. O'Neil was concerned about the girls appearing, even fully dressed, because of the nature of their work and its possible reflection on the program standards of CBS. But he didn't think the censors would object to their conductor.

Jacques Goldetsky met with O'Neil that very afternoon.

"Are you doing this for music's sake or for shock value?" asked the Goodson-Todman interviewer of Larry as he took several Polaroid shots of him.

"Do you think I would spend all these years practicing, just to take off my shirt?" Larry answered boldly with a French-Italian accent that was purposely muddled. He was suddenly concerned that the interviewer might have a linguist handy who could pin him down in whatever language "Jacques Goldetsky" spoke. His outfit for this occasion was a tam, swagger stick, monocle and some music manuscript.

"Just what is your native tongue, Mr. Goldetsky?"

"It's a gypsy language," Larry ad-libbed. "One of forty dialects which only two hundred people in the world speak."

"Can you tell me how the topless habit began with your ensemble?"

"Well, it was all accidental. We were practicing in Paris. It was a terribly hot day and one of the girls took off her blouse. Then another took off her blouse. I took off my shirt. Our first violinist loosened her brassiere. The violist took hers off. I removed my undershirt. The cellist took off her sweater and bra, even her skirt."

The interviewer cleared his throat in a manner that suggested some embarrassment. "And then what happened?" he asked with pretended disinterest.

"Well, the girls realized they could play more freely without bras and I found I was happier stripped to the waist."

The interview ended and Larry thought he was completely believed. Anyway the fellow never challenged his credibility during the half-hour, or even laughed, although Larry had said many funny things. The questions seemed well prepared and very routine. To Larry it was like delivering comedy lines to a computer.

In any event, Jacques Goldetsky was asked to stand by for a definite booking date.

Meantime, the girls' photo started to stimulate more interest from the press. Calls came in from the Philadelphia *Evening Bulletin,* the Chicago *Daily News* and Reuters News Service. They all requested personal interviews with the girls and tickets to their first New York concert. I promised to keep everybody informed.

The San Francisco *Chronicle* was the first actually to

run the photograph of the girls, bare breasts peeking from behind their instruments. Centered under the heading "Picture of the Week" in the Sunday edition, it was all the more amusing flanked on either side by the columns of Walter Lippmann and James Reston. Head shots of both men looked sternly toward the revealing photograph.

Record companies suddenly discovered the First Topless String Quartet. Frank Sinatra wrote me a note and expressed interest in recording the girls for an album on his Reprise label. I replied that the jacket cover alone would sell a million copies. Then Jubilee records had the same idea; Richard Gersh, an independent record promotion man, became interested in the quartet for one of the many companies he represented. I didn't pursue these interests and they soon died out. After all, our girls could only appear, they didn't play.

Famous Faces, Inc., a pop poster outfit, considered the girls for a huge poster that would sell for a dollar or two. But they changed their minds and wrote a letter saying: "We've decided it's not our bag."

A letter arrived from Brooke Maddux, assistant editor with *McCall's* magazine, saying: "Thank you for thinking of *McCall's* for an article on The First Topless String Quartet. It was certainly an original thought! I'm sure that the four young ladies are thoroughly delightful and their musicianship impeccable. But somehow, I don't think the material would be suitable for *McCall's*. String quartets are a little highbrow for mass appeal, don't you think?"

David Bourdon from *Life* magazine called and asked for the negatives on our girls' photos. They were going ahead with the story after all, he said, and the material was needed as fast as a messenger could rush it over. It was very brave of them, I thought, as I donned my messenger's uniform and raced to the Time & Life building with the negatives. That was June 6, 1967. But they didn't use the story until four months later in their October 13 issue. It was an in-depth treatment on national nudity by Paul O'Neil, who commented seriously on a "Bach-with-breasts by the First Topless String Quartet." But there were no pictures.

I called Bourdon and he explained, "The original layout had photos of your quartet in very prominent positions, but somebody high in editorial killed the visuals."

He felt that by eliminating the photographs *Life* had evaded the article's intent—to expose the nudity craze—and I agreed.

Life's article printed my Fifth Avenue address and the broom closet was soon loaded with requests for interviews, personal appearances and autographed photographs. At that point we had just about spent our maximum budget of $250, so this batch of mail was going to have to remain unanswered.

I happened to tune in on Johnny Carson's *Tonight* show about this time and his sub, Jimmy Dean, held up a photograph of the girls, very briefly. Laughing, Dean commented that he found it hard to believe, so he just had to show it. And then he did again, in full view of millions.

Whenever something like this happens on TV, Jeanne and I receive calls from friends who are dying to know if the personality is in on the joke. We keep telling them over and over they're not; my experience has been that when the star of a show knows he's being put on, he won't do the same to his audience unless there is a "confession" before the show ends. Almost always, though, he has to be fooled or the gag will never be aired.

Eddie Fisher showed some interest in the First Topless String Quartet. He was in the middle of a recording session with forty musicians when he spied the girls' photo on Norman Forrest's music stand. Fisher stopped the orchestra mid-song and came over for a closer look. So did everybody else, much to Forrest's amusement, and it wasn't long before music circles buzzed about "the four swinging chicks with fiddles besides."

Steve Allen called from Hollywood and offered to put the girls on camera, sans tops, if they would pay their own way to the Coast. I agreed if Steve would reciprocate by coming to New York and appear on stage, nude, with the girls. He wouldn't do it.

A Miss Taubman from the New York *Post* requested information on the quartet for an article she was preparing. She was particularly interested in the background of second violinist Gretchen Gansebrust. I explained that the word "gansebrust" mean "breast of goose" in Swedish. She never questioned its unlikelihood as a name. But then most people don't question the zany things I say. And no one ever questioned why a string quartet had *five* members! For that matter, quartets just don't have conductors, shirtless or otherwise.

A letter appeared in *Life*'s letters-to-the-editor column the week after their story on the First Topless String Quartet:

Dear Sirs:

Regarding your article on nudity I found it most interesting. Especially since I recently witnessed a concert by The First Topless String Quartet on an estate near London. I was amazed at the amount of excitement aroused by the four young female semi-nude musicians from the black tie audience of four or five hundred people, mostly men. They laughed and jeered and made some rude sexual sounds from time to time. It was certainly out of keeping with the social setting!

Afterwards the host told me she thought it was going to be a "fun" experience to have such a Saturday concert, but "never again!" Her carefully screened guests originally numbered about a hundred and fifty. But numerous uninvited ones mobbed her gardens and trampled her dahlias and much of the shrubbery was beyond repair. Some of the younger people even carved naughty words on the door of the bath house!

Personally I don't believe there is anything wrong with nudity per se, but when it is exploited for personal glorification as with this First Topless String Quartet, then I say shame, shame, shame!

Yours sincerely,
(Miss) A. G.

Naturally I had written this letter. But though I confess its fabrication, I've met people who insist they attended that particular social function or others where the First Topless String Quartet performed!

Life was kind enough to forward all the mail they were receiving for the quartet, much of it from "artists" living in West Virginia, the Ozarks and Oklahoma. This one from a chap in Fox, Oklahoma, was typical:

Dear Sirs:

I am a artist and I drew picture of rivers and mountains but now I am starting to drew people. If you can send me 14 pictures of nude men and some women I can start learning to drew them. Please tell me how much.

Sincerely yours,
G.H.

By the end of 1967 I had forgotten about the First Topless String Quartet, what with my lectures and writing assignments. But along came comedian Woody Allen, who talked about our quartet on his *Kraft Music Hall* television special December 27. He made reference to his not caring much for their allegretto movement, but said, "When the music played 'presto alle brave' I really got excited!"

In the January 1968 issue of *Esquire* magazine, the First Topless String Quartet was voted that magazine's Dubious Achievement Award for the year. They published the photograph of "Jacques Goldetsky" conducting the girls —all topless—and captioned it with, "Yeah, but wait till you see 'The Flight of the Bumblebee'!"

Mail continued to arrive at the broom closet in a daily deluge, not only from more artists in residence but college students who wanted personally autographed photographs of the girls. However, all they were destined to receive was this form letter:

Suite 320

507 Fifth Avenue

New York, N.Y. 10017

(212) OXford 7-5895

IMPORTANT: When replying
refer to Code #7368250974

Dear Person:

This is a form letter. I am unable to answer you personally because the cost in time is prohibitive. Allow me to illustrate:

PROCEDURE	TIME
Opening and reading your letter	3 minutes
Thinking up an answer to your letter	4 "
Dictating letter to my secretary	16 "

PROCEDURE		TIME
Locating stationery, inserting into typewriter, typing an original and two carbons, removing from typewriter, separating carbons and onion skin copies.	18	,,
Reading, correcting and signing	9	,,
Licking, sealing and stamping	1	,,
Delivering to mailbox	3	,,
Returning from mailbox	6	,,
TOTAL:	60 minutes	

(BASED UPON THE NEW YORK STATE MINIMUM HOURLY WAGE SCALE OF $1.60, AN HOUR OF MY TIME, PLUS THE SAME FOR MY SECRETARY, COMES TO $3.20)

Therefore, if you wish to receive a personal reply, please forward $3.50 by certified check, cash or money order. (The extra 30 cents is for stationery, envelope, carbon, onion skin and postage.)

Meantime, as a temporary reply to your initial inquiry, let me say: _____yes __✓__no _____maybe

> Sincerely,
> Alan Abel
> Occupant

P.S. Please do not ask for an open account unless you are rated in D.&B.

The nationally syndicated *Alan Burke Show* was a natural platform on which to gain a final blast of television exposure for the quartet and spoof nudity, sex and censorship—which was really the initial basis for our topless hoax. So I made my way over to his regular Thursday night taping session, armed with the photograph of the girls that had appeared in *Esquire* Magazine.

Burke's producer recognized me from previous appearances as a strange character with loony causes and seemed eager to place me near the head of the line. In front of me, also waiting to speak to Alan Burke, were three men. One had an accordion and was holding his mother's hand, another had a bird cage that was empty, and the third was a tall, lanky chap with a bow and arrow.

After the audience filed in and the lights went up, I was motioned to go on first:

"My name is Dr. Bruce Spencer, Mr. Burke, and I am a sex scientist."

Burke looked at me curiously but did not show any sign of recognition. He said sarcastically that I looked like a sex scientist and asked me about my work.

"For the past six months I have been in a cold laboratory studying human sexual response," I explained. "We invited young ladies in, had them talk and secretly recorded their conversations. We learned that 18 per cent of the girls in this country today would like to be prostitutes. I am recommending to Congress that we legalize prostitution. Why? Because it's the oldest business in the world. And it's done quite well for itself! With the cost of living and taxes going sky high, where can an honest, hard-working girl get a job where she doesn't have to report all her income to the government? Now you don't seem too very disturbed by what I'm telling you, Mr. Burke."

Burke fiendishly replied that the only thing disturbing him was the fact I was disturbed.

"Well, I am. That's why I'm *here!*" I answered pointedly as the audience laughed and applauded with glee.

"Also, I'm doing a survey on nudists, trying to give them a clean bill of health. Nudists are always being castigated. What's wrong with a nudist? Their colonies have developed some of the finest volleyball players in the country. Last summer I myself sang tenor with the Altoona, Pennsylvania, All Nudist Choir. I met some very interesting sopranos and altos. Of course there were a few showoffs among the baritones who did a lot of running and jumping. . . ."

"Doctor, aren't you a sex maniac?" interrupted Burke.

"I was an Eagle Scout, I served in the army, I'm a paid up member of the Moose," I protested lamely. "I am only interested in sex because I want to fill a void . . . to prove my point that permissiveness is popular. I would like to show you a photograph that appeared in *Esquire*. This is a group of four nudists who are culturally inclined. It's the First Topless String Quartet. Now these four girls actually play together. Don't laugh. Also, Mr. Burke, I'd like to see everybody in this audience eventually take a lesbian to lunch. Why not? They're nice people. They're not all truck drivers. They don't all operate fork lifts. . . ."

Burke ended the discussion with a wave of his hand for the next guest and said to me, "I'd like to have you back again when you're prepared to divulge more than you obviously will divulge now."

This particular encounter with Alan Burke was broadcast over WNEW-TV on Saturday, February 17, 1968, and was responsible for another outpouring of mail to my broom closet. One hate letter addressed simply to "Nude Quartet with Girls, New York City" found its way to me. Yes, the post office has quite a file on my nefarious activities and knows my address.

Finally, a Swedish newspaper, *Kvallsposten*, published one of the rehearsal photos of the quartet. It showed Jacques very deadpan between two of the girls looking over some sheet music. They were all grouped around a piano. Holding up his baton as if to set the rhythm, he looked more nude than the girls—with only his bow tie and cummerbund. The accompanying story quoted my press releases and was headlined "Opus Sex!" If anyone had taken a magnifying glass to the picture, they might have discerned the music Goldetsky was conducting. Its title: "I've Got a Lovely Bunch of Coconuts."

NINETEEN

HOW TO COPE WITH ROBBERS, SALESMEN AND FUND RAISERS

Hoaxing has some practical applications, too. Our Upper Westside apartment in Manhattan has this warning printed on our front door in English, Spanish and Hebrew:

> THIEVES BEWARE!
> This apartment is protected by a 45 megaton cobalt bomb. If you use more than *one pound* of pressure against this door, the bomb is guaranteed by the manufacturer to explode. NOTE: If the bomb happens to go off accidentally, you must seek medical aid within 24 hours.

Since my wife and I live in a very high crime-rate area—New York City—and our apartment is on the ground floor, we are particularly vulnerable to roving bands of thieves. They read the bomb notice and leave us alone. (We've watched them through our peephole!) Even a hardened criminal will balk at breaking into a place where, apparently, a mad bomber lives. Fear is the best weapon against crime, I'm convinced, because our apartment remains the only one in the building that hasn't been forcibly entered through the front door.

Several tenants in our building complained to the superintendent about the wisdom of our keeping a deadly bomb on the premises. He tried to convince them that it was only a ruse and there was nothing to worry about. But they were still apprehensive.

A salesman rang our bell one morning and complained about the bomb notice: "I was leaning against your door with at least *two* pounds of pressure talking to a friend. Why, the damn thing could have gone off and I'd be killed!" he said angrily.

"No danger, fellow," I replied calmly. "You were perfectly safe. We only connect the bomb to explode after midnight."

He grudgingly grunted that he understood and gave me a dirty look as he walked away.

The back door to our apartment leads into a rear hallway that connects with the fire exit. We have our door fitted with a dead bolt lock and a crossbar that make it impregnable against every type of assault except perhaps a pneumatic drill or acetylene torch. About 4 A.M. one morning Jeanne heard some scratching at the back door and she woke me up. I listened and obviously someone was trying to trip the lock with a celluloid strip.

There was no point in calling the police because by the time they came he would be gone. And it wouldn't take him much longer to realize his mission was impossible. Meanwhile, I decided to give the intruder a psychological warning he would never forget. I slipped quietly into our living room and removed from the wall a Chinese gong along with its mallet, made of hard rubber. The gong was three feet in diameter and had once been used to sound a battle charge—at least that's what the fellow in the antique shop told me.

Just inches from the back door where the celluloid strip was probing, I took a firm stance and motioned for Jeanne to hold her ears. Then I wacked the gong once as loud as I could. The noise was deafening. There was a muffled scream, the sound of tools being scattered, the patter of tennis shoes out the rear fire exit, up over a ten-foot spiked fence, a *thud* as he dropped to the sidewalk, and the echo of fast-running feet as he raced down the block.

Another ruse Jeanne and I employ when walking in our neighborhood is to dress like muggers. By dressing down—my wife wears a moth-eaten coat she bought at a rummage sale for three dollars and I have a tattered overcoat that died on a Robert Hall pipe rack twenty years ago—we look pretty desperate ourselves. Even the panhandlers tend to leave us alone. And when one does approach us, I whip out my ball-point pen and attempt to sell it to him. Or Jeanne will talk to me with high school Italian while I answer her in elementary French. Only once did a beggar outfox us by suddenly speaking to me in perfect French. I gave him a quarter.

Since my wife and I do a lot of traveling for lectures around the country, it is impossible to subscribe to magazines. Nevertheless, we receive our share of telephone calls from magazine salesmen when we are home. No explanation short of hanging up rudely seems to prevent them from launching into their prepared sales pitches. I've tried the honest approach: "I'm just not home enough to subscribe to *anything*." But they go right on and I'm stuck listening, kicking myself for being trapped.

I've never hung up on any salesman, although plenty have done so to me ever since I developed this basic response:

> You say you're selling *Life* magazine? No, I'm not interested because I don't approve of George Hunt. Who's he? He's the managing editor. Now how can you possibly interest anyone in a magazine when you don't even know who the editor is! Look, fellow, I'm very busy; if you must know I'm giving a blood transfusion. Is this a recording? All right, all right, I can't stand to listen to any more of your sob story. I'll take a free trial and the free gift. I'm a traveling salesman so start the subscription February 29 in care of the Statler Hotel in Cleveland, Ohio. A week later, the Palmer House in Chicago; the following week I'll be at the Westbury Hotel in Toronto—hello, hello. I say, where are you?

I always get cut off at that point. If not, I have a handy list of fifteen more cities and hotels at the ready. The salesman can't afford to waste much time on a dismal prospect like me!

Another routine I use for aggressive telephone salesmen offering free trial photographs, dancing lessons for life, burial plots or over-the-counter stocks goes like this:

> I'm just not interested. I know it's a good deal. It's not that I can't pay either. Yes, I have the money. Well, you'd have to send the bill to my lawyer. You see I just received a 3- to 10-year sentence at Sing Sing for assault with a deadly weapon and attempt to kill. Actually I'm innocent; my

lawyer is making an appeal and he handles all my money matters. Thanks for calling and good luck to you, too!

Both Jeanne and I like to donate to charities when we know for certain that a large portion of the money actually goes to the cause itself and not the fund-raising organization. I am somewhat suspicious of the casual doorbell ringer—usually a sad-faced woman in her sixties, shabbily dressed, with a can in her hand—or the telephone solicitor who requests that a donation be sent to a post-office box number.

In each instance I make a simple request: "I would like to come down to your office with my accountant and go over your books, not out of mistrust but because it's my policy. Just as a bank never loans anybody a dime until they produce a good credit rating, this is my way of determining whether or not I should make a sizable donation to your cause."

No charity has ever been willing to accept a donation from me on these terms! Naturally I would never take the time and money necessary to go over an organization's books and records; I would just write out a check. But nobody has ever called my bluff. That's why we donate to small and obscure nonprofit charities who don't engage in national advertising, telethons or personal solicitations.

Only recently the bomb notice on our front door had to come off. Too many complaints from the tenants and visitors to the building. So we replaced it with a sign that reads: "Premises Protected by Attack Dog."

When our doorbell rings a Doberman pinscher snarls with the most vicious and threatening sounds such a dog can make. But it's only a tape recording that lasts one minute and resets itself. One of our relatives dropped by unexpectedly a year ago while we were out of town, rang the doorbell and hasn't returned since. She still insists we have a dangerous dog on the premises and refuses to believe anything to the contrary.

As I say, hoaxing has its practical applications.

TWENTY

SO WHAT NEXT?

Occasionally I decide to stop enjoying myself and to resign my life to something more socially acceptable. Then I get some last-minute reprieve. Like last week when ad man David Bascom called me from San Francisco; he needed a green moose.

"How about a pink one?" I asked.

"No, it has to be green on account of it's intended to walk on New York's Fifth Avenue in the St. Patrick's Day Parade."

"Would a deer do?" I asked. "Or maybe a papier-mâché imitation? How about two guys in a horse suit?"

"No. It has to be full grown, antlers and all. A live moose, male. And green."

I had once worked for Bascom on the West Coast as an advertising copywriter and his particular joy in life is the creation of unusual ideas. On the side, he publishes a satirical monthly newspaper, *The Wretched Mess,* and a yearly calendar that names a crazy celebration for each day of the year. For example: "National Constipation Day," "Kick a Computer Day," "Typographical Eror Day," "Hell Freezes Over Day" and other such nonsense.

I called all the theatrical animal rental agencies in the Yellow Pages. But none of them happened to have a moose on hand.

Bascom had explained that the moose represents the trademark of the Skyline TV-radio network in the northwestern part of the United States and they were to sponsor the animal's entry in the parade. Most important, it had to be painted green.

It was my wife who finally nipped the thing in the bud. "Isn't spring the mating season for moose?" she asked. "I think it was some Walt Disney movie where I remember that from. The male moose gets very hostile."

I called Bascom with the bad news, which he accepted graciously, and he offered me another assignment—to deliver the booby prize to a contest winner in New York.

"Sure," I said, ever ready to put on my messenger's uniform and make a delivery. "What's the prize?"

"A ton of gravel," he advised.

"A ton of gravel! Dave, couldn't you just have some local construction company do that?"

Then he explained that it wasn't as simple as it sounded. The winner, a girl, had insisted that the prize be delivered to a boy friend's apartment. He was soon to return from a trip abroad and she wanted to surprise him by dumping the ton of gravel in his living room!

After calling construction companies and talking to a lot of guys who sounded as if they had gravel in their throats, and thought I was crazy, I found a solution. Since this whole thing was only a gag, the sacks wouldn't even need to contain gravel. I'd just stuff them with paper, hire actors to do the delivering, and have them stagger in with the bags. The plan was all set to go.

But at the zero hour, the girl chickened out. She decided to have a real ton of gravel sent to a friend in the country who needed a driveway.

Sometimes I am asked to gate-crash a party or event, pretending I'm some royal figure or other. I flatly refuse such an assignment unless it has been prearranged with the host or sponsor. Personally, I see no purpose in stealing past private guards just to gain entrance someplace I haven't been invited. There are plenty of unemployed second-story men around more than eager to perform such feats. It's just not my gag bag.

The late Stan Berman made a practice of gate crashing and earned a national reputation for his entries into the Presidential box at President John F. Kennedy's Inaugural Ball, the New York ticker tape parade for astronaut John Glenn, and the 1962 Academy Awards on national television when he walked across the stage with an Oscar.

I was always fascinated by Berman's audacity and the skill with which he was able to infiltrate maximum security defenses at such important events. Hopefully, security officials learned something about the weaknesses of their defenses and the necessity of challenging everybody on the premises, paying as much attention to the person in a fancy suit as well as the innocent electrician in baggy pants.

In the fall of 1967 when I was writing a humor column for the Washington (D.C.) *Examiner,* I received an invitation to attend the Lynda Bird Johnson–Captain Charles Robb wedding in the White House. Just to walk up to the door of that big white house is an awesome experience. Seeing how stringent the security was, I must say I was a bit hesitant about going in.

After all, there was the picketing in front of the White House I had done a few years before in the name of animal decency. And then I'd run my own candidate for President of the United States who wasn't old enough to be sworn in. Also, I'd come to challenge the investigatory talents of the C.I.A., the F.B.I., the Secret Service and Drew Pearson. I figured the guards might have some skeptical notions about me.

As I surrendered the letter of invitation and my description was radioed to a central headquarters somewhere, I saw a dozen members of the Marine Corps string ensemble stroll unchallenged past the guards with their instruments. Now if I were a White House guard I would have perceived them the true threat to security, not me. What if they were foreign agents who had kidnaped the real musicians and now had machine guns in their violin cases? I hadn't read Dick Tracy all those years without picking up a few tricks!

It took a little time to clear my identity. I had a press card in the name of Prof. Bunker C. Hill, a driver's license in my real name and a union card listing me as Bruce Spencer. But I finally made it.

And what did I see as I strolled across the White House lawn? President Johnson's dog Yuki decently clothed in a suit and socks! One of the handlers told me the costume had been put on for the President's amusement only, that's all.

Noticing reporter Marjorie Hunter from *The New York Times* nearby, I asked her if she remembered "those nuts who picketed the White House for the sake of animal decency several years ago."

"I certainly do," she replied. "I kept getting mail from them and some kind of certificate saying I was something or other."

"That was probably their S.I.N.A. Achievement Award," I suggested. "It was given to all reporters who wrote front-page stories on their movement. I was down here that day, too, and it seemed like the whole Washington press corps turned out."

"They certainly did," she said.

"Do you think those people are serious, like religious fanatics?" I asked.

"I think so," Miss Hunter replied. "But I think there is something screwy, too. I think they just have money."

It seemed to me that she still didn't know it was all a gag. Nor did Miss Hunter recognize me as the picket she had interviewed when I posed as "a former used-tire salesman who had at last found a purpose in life by clothing all naked animals."

I can't pretend it takes much prompting for me to put people on. It's sort of instinctive. I see an opportunity for comedy in just about every life situation. And so do my close friends. When writer Buck Henry and I used to work together—before his recent film successes with *The Graduate, Candy* and *Catch-22*—we might have been on a bus going crosstown in Manhattan, talking shop, and suddenly notice that other passengers were tuned in on our conversation. We couldn't resist improvising:

"Before I forget, Buck, I received a letter from my grandmother today. She's up for parole shortly."

"How many times did she shoot her lover in the groin?"

"Six times. He was an hermaphrodite. So she had to kill all the organs."

"Wicked woman," Buck said angrily. "If she hadn't plastered that plumber with goose grease, he'd be alive, too!"

"Yes," I remarked sadly. "Funny how he was hooked on her dill pickles. And to think one of them exploded internally. Most people just aren't aware of the power of a homemade pickle when it tangles with the digestive juices."

"Stupid fool he was. Took the pickle anally. And to think an obstetrician gave him the wrong diagnosis!"

By the time we reached our stop, every passenger within hearing distance had become totally involved in our conversation. We always left them dangling with a final *non sequitur*: ". . . and so I wanted to warn the Mayor because granny sent one of her pickles to *his* wife."

Another time we were riding down the elevator in my office building with a talkative woman, a character I recognized as being the same one who had been evicted from the restaurant next door for selling Irish Sweepstakes tickets from table to table. She now took the opportunity to try to sell us a hundred wind-up musical crosses that played "Come to Jesus" and a mailing list of five hundred people in Alabama who she swore would buy anything religious.

"How can I be certain the people on your mailing list

are not deadbeats?" I asked, while Buck and my wife maintained straight faces.

"Deadbeats? Such a bad word! Listen, Bubala, you can trust me like a mother. Would your mother lie to you? Don't I remind you a little of your own mother? Tell me the truth."

"Well, there is a vague resemblance, but . . ."

"You see! You recognize in me your own mother. So how could I lie to such a sweet person? Buy the list. Take a few crosses. I'll trust you for 25 per cent down and I'll carry the balance for a few pennies a day. I have my own credit deal. Here! In my purse is a contract . . ."

We were now standing on the sidewalk with a small crowd listening as she went on and on. I just surrendered to the madness of the scene while trying not to laugh. Then I became aware of bubbles passing in front of me, past the woman's face. It was Buck. He was blowing bubbles off his tongue and she never even noticed them, building her sales pitch as she was, to a wild frenzy.

I've often been asked why I don't just write and perform in comedy sketches on television shows and forget hoaxing. It would indeed be more remunerative to channel my ideas into a medium that is at the same time socially rewarding. But I've resisted many offers along these lines. Mostly because even the most satirical comedy sketches on the tube have no lasting impact. They are, by their very identification with TV, viewed passively and then forgotten. And when the censor gets done editing there's even less to remember. Quickly, now, can you recall the subject matter of a funny routine on any of last week's television shows? Last month's? Last year's? Ever?

Another question people constantly ask me is, "Have you ever been arrested for one of your hoaxes?" And the answer is, "Of course not!" It is not my intention to violate the law. Or do anything I consider to be in bad taste. My purpose is always to amuse and poke fun. The initial idea has to be inherently humorous and make a satirical point besides. If there is ever any danger of hurting somebody, I won't get involved.

I am appalled by some of the so-called practical joking I hear about. An assistant personnel director laughingly told me he once was screening new junior executives for his boss when he recognized a former college classmate. After they exchanged hellos he advised the guy to salute his boss, remain stiffly at attention during the interview and back out of the office when finished.

The poor fellow did exactly as told and was dismissed abruptly by the VIP, who, when later told about the joke, was terribly annoyed. He had liked the applicant's record and—except for his stiff military bearing and "other strange behavior"—would have considered him for the job, but by then it was already filled.

When a New York producer for whom I worked was having difficulties renewing his building lease, he asked me to threaten his landlord as though I might be a member of the Mafia. I explained to him that I didn't do that sort of impractical joking. Not only could I be arrested for violating the law (there must be one for impersonating a Mafia member!), but the real Mafia might find out, get angry and go after Flicker himself. Or maybe even me.

Although I have never been arrested, I must confess I always half expect to be tapped on the shoulder by a policeman when pulling one of my stunts. So far, though,

I've found the men in blue to be pretty nice in the face of the madness I create. One exception was after I lectured to the members of a Malvern, Long Island, mystery club. I took some of them out on the street to prove how easy it was to obtain signatures from pedestrians on a phony petition.

My co-conspirator, Arnold Lasky, tried to persuade a foot patrolman to sign the paper headed "Ease the Population Explosion." But when the officer read the declaration he angrily started to give our group a summons for "disturbing the peace and unlawful assembly." Only Arnold's being an attorney, which he eventually pointed out, saved the situation. The petition read:

EASE THE POPULATION EXPLOSION
We the undersigned, in order to help decentralize urban areas, hereby declare ourselves to be of unsound minds, unnecessary as citizens, and urgently petition the proper authorities to commit us to the nearest available shelter for people with similar problems.

Needless to say, the fun business has its shortcomings. Some people just don't take kindly to my having fun at their expense. They are usually shocked after having been hoodwinked by one of my roles; later they'll feel foolish over their gullibility. Most of us don't like to be fooled. Even in fun it's a blow to the ego that our power of perception was not quite as sharp as we always thought it to be.

We're supposed to put aside our toys at the age of consent. And with them our imagination and spirit of adventure. "Why don't you grow up and act your age?" is a sign of this disapproval. I don't accept such an admonishment. To me, it goes hand in hand with "Don't fold, spindle or bend," "Keep off the grass," "No ball playing," "Blot—don't rub" and other such infringements on my civil rights.

Yet those people who pursue only the sane and sensible things in life don't seem to be enjoying themselves very much. When was the last time you saw a banker smile? Or a lawyer laugh? I think that only if you enjoy your life's work—whether it be the making of crank shafts, running a restaurant or inventing jokes—can your life have meaning to you or to others. Plodding along, doing what is expected, without faith or fun, can be a pretty dull way to spend the few years any one person has on this planet.

A put-on is not necessarily a put-down. I liken what I do sometimes to a life game, as an adventure in absurdity, an adult fairytale in which I engage people emotionally and intellectually. The audience gets involved and has to decide for itself what's going on and what's to be learned from the experience. Everybody is a participant.

I like to think people will learn something from my hijinks; that they will become a little more cautious before accepting and believing everything they read or hear or see. Because the next time around their hoaxer might truly be diabolical and rob them of things far more important and meaningful.

Several years ago I addressed a group of fraternity students at the University of British Columbia, posing as a recruiter for a private foundation. This particular spoof had been arranged by a campus director of entertainment, Murray Farr, who wanted to shake up the students a bit. They had already been subjected to several weeks of interviews by executives from major oil companies, computer concerns and other big business operations that like to sweep down on campuses and grab the cream of the seniors.

A huge living room in the fraternity-owned mansion was the setting and it overflowed with several hundred students. I answered their questions for nearly an hour.

"I'd like to know how much you earn as vice-president of the Spencer Research Foundation," asked one clean-cut, well-dressed youth.

I hadn't explained the kind of work Spencer Research did, except to hint we were in "highly secret intramural consultation analysis."

"First let me say that my salary runs approximately fifteen thousand a year plus expenses and I might add that I pick up an extra fifteen hundred dollars or so by handing in a fairly well-padded swindle sheet."

"What do you actually do?" asked the same voice.

"Nothing. I attend the luncheons my boss doesn't care to go to. I pick up his plaques and awards, suffer through the cold roast beef and make a little speech telling everybody how wonderful they are. I don't like my work at all. In fact, I hate it. But I do it for the money."

"Are there other benefits?" someone asked.

"Some. Besides health insurance, paid vacations and two more daily coffee breaks than General Motors gives its employees, the keys to our washrooms are gold-plated. After the summer picnics I get to take home all the extra wieners and beer my wife and I can carry."

The students and their dates laughed heartily at my deadpan delivery, enjoying my apparently *laissez-faire* attitude toward life. No one asked what he could offer to the company. The obligation was one way only. Their line of questioning revealed they had come to expect a life hermetically sealed, guaranteed and insured.

"But where are *you* headed for?" asked a sweet young girl with dismay in her voice.

"Nowhere," I replied gloomily. "I'm on a treadmill. There is no future with my company. You grab what you can when you can. I take home all the rubber bands, paper clips and pencils I can hide in my attaché case. Well, I have a little office-supply mail-order business on the side. To help support my mother.

"Finally, let me say this. Our foundation gives me and every employee who stays at least ten years his own private burial plot overlooking the Hudson River—large enough for a family of four and two pets. Also, a funeral fit for a chairman of the board, and perpetual grave care, which would include flowers every Veterans Day for me—or on Thanksgiving Day if you were a Conscientious Objector. And I'd like to see I.B.M. or A.T.&T. top that!"

I left a bewildered group, without explaining that their legs had been pulled, because I was running late for a radio talk show that evening with Bob Newhart. They didn't learn that it was a joke until the next day, midway during my SINA lecture in front of the entire student body. The timing of my revelation was propitious. Unknown to me, a group of boys from the fraternity, who had been angered by my pompous attitude the night before, were backstage ready to toss me into the swimming pool. When I confessed the hoax, they went sheepishly back to their seats.

I no longer try to defend my role as a professional hoaxer. Many people understand and approve of the things I do. To rationalize my life games is an affront to their intelligence and their ready sense of humor. And to try to make friends with those who are infuriated by my wacky crusades, well, they are all the more offended if I try to explain myself.

Most of what I do would be considered comedy *if* it were announced as such before I performed. But even on a TV show, audiences to whom I haven't been introduced in comedy terms have again and again been fooled. They will laugh, all right. But most are laughing *at* me, not with me. They've rejected the mirror image I've extended to them because it's more comfortable to dismiss me as a nut.

Some people who might otherwise enjoy the satire—if it were within the recognizable format of a TV variety show—simply linger in doubt about what I am doing. Even a subsequent explanation that my performance was a hoax eludes them, as borne out by the hate mail I receive following a television appearance.

P. T. Barnum made a fortune feeding his customers one sort of humbug after another. Although today we think ourselves much more sophisticated and learned than our ancestors, I am convinced we are nonetheless gullible in the face of the Big Lies and just as vulnerable to being taken. We all want to believe. The more preposterous the story, the more we want it to be true.

I can't say I blame people for becoming brainwashed, passive cogs, in an increasingly technical age. For we are constantly barraged by and glutted with so much propaganda and product advertising that our senses have grown dull to it all. But we are the consumers. And the function of the consumer is to consume and throw away. Our economy depends on it.

In spite of our reliance on theater reviewers to tell us what to see, the *Good Housekeeping* Seal of Approval to tell us what to buy or canned laughter to tell us when to laugh, I still can't bear to think people will surrender their individuality and with it the right to make up their own minds.

I wonder for whose benefit we have censorship. As soon as a book is banned, it's increased sales are assured. When a remark is blipped from a late night TV show, you wonder what for? The kids are long since in bed, or should be. And if their health is being ruined by keeping them up after midnight, a few four-letter words won't matter.

Are the scissor biddies protecting us adults lest we hear a naughty or profane word? It's the bleeping out of a word that really makes it indecent. Words or comments that might have passed unnoticed suddenly become more noticeable, and obscene, by their ommision.

When Alan Burke finally learned that I was a professional hoaxer, he hired me to come on his show in late December, 1968, pretending to be the general manager of his station, WNEW-TV, with a forecast of programming for the new year, 1969. One of my predictions was that "this Metromedia station will compete with *Laugh-In* and other highly rated programs on opposing stations by offering live bingo games direct from St. Patrick's Cathedral."

Their censor deleted this comment from the tape. But he overlooked a chart I showed with a penis-like curve. I found it difficult to believe that I'd be censored on a show that airs Madeline Murray, homosexuals, exile priests and all manner of strange people. Apparently, you can say or show anything outrageous, as long as it's done seriously. But say it with humor and it's suddenly suspect.

If I had lived a few hundred years ago, I guess I'd have been a court jester, inventing stories and performing funny feats to make people laugh and forget their problems. Back in the old days there was the bubonic plague and crazy kings and a nonexistent sewage system that was as much a hazard to unsuspecting pedestrians as runaway horses. But can our present-day society, hedonistic as it is, totally concerned with material accumulation, fouling its air with poisons, killing and maiming, be any less in need of humor?

What does a fellow with the instincts of a court jester do when he finds himself in a fast-paced, mechanized age, in an overstimulated society preoccupied with its search for a guaranteed underarm deodorant and a cancer-free cigarette? What can a court jester do who is born to the Hydrogen Age in a country that has no court and no royalty? Not in this Administration anyway.

Our society deems it far more sensible to be a doctor, more prestigious to be an astronaut and more lucrative to sell insurance than it is to pursue a life work of making fun. Nevertheless, I continue to hoax, and, from time to time, do my put-on "thing" as a paid performer in order to earn a livelihood and protect the creative independence that hoaxing demands.

I receive about one speaking inquiry a week, mostly from offbeat but legitimate organizations looking for an unusual entertainer:

Dear Mr. Spencer:

I understand that you are the agent for Professor Otto Von Schottenstubble of Vienna. If he is not too expensive I would like to have him lecture at the American Frac-

ture Association Meeting between November 9–13, 1969
at the Sheraton-Columbus Hotel, Columbus, Ohio.

It has been rumored that the Professor had a rather
unfortunate experience when he injected himself with
the serum from a laughing hyena and is still suffering
from the effects. Of course we all remember his tremendous success in warding off syphilis by injecting the troops
with malaria before they went into red light districts
when on leave.

We certainly hope that Professor Schottenstubble,
Ph.D., M.D., B.B.S., A.S.S., will be in the country so I can
arrange for his appearance at our banquet as the honored
speaker.

> Very truly yours,
> C. L., M.D.

Dear Doctor:

Thank you for your letter of January 27. Unfortunately, Professor Otto Von Schottenstubble will be in
Mexico next November completing his research on the
dreaded blastomycosis that affected Governor George
Wallace and General Curtis LeMay. And the good Professor is still behind on 3857 pregnancy tests!

So this leaves us only with Dr. Hugo Hindemith (no
relation to the composer) from Switzerland, who will be
visiting the U.S.A. next November under my exclusive
management.

Dr. Hindemith is a former proctologist who switched
to ophthalmology when his psychiatrist recommended a
complete change of scenery. You may have read his book
The Ape and You.

His stimulating forty-minute lecture is concerned with
psychosomatic diseases and their relationship to bedside
manners. He also touches on sexy innovations too discreet
to disclose through the U.S. mails.

Dr. Hindemith has a set fee of $750 (including free
typhus injections for those in need right on stage) plus
$250 for incidental expenses that would include traveling,

food, housing, charts, instruments, medical supplies and molds.

Looking forward to hearing from you, I remain

Sincerely yours,
Bruce Spencer

And occasionally I open my mail and find a fan letter:

Dear Alan,

I saw you on the Johnny Carson show last night. I stayed up to watch and you looked good. But where do you go from here? When I think of all the years you've been fooling around with jokes. You could have been a doctor and maybe even a lawyer by now!

There is still time to go back to college and succeed. Think about it. Stay well and write all the news.

Love,
Mother

P.S. What is Johnny Carson really like? Could you get four tickets in May for his show? Mr. and Mrs. Ackerman are coming to New York on a tour and they were so kind (she brought over some apple strudel yesterday) it's the least we can do for them. They were both so thrilled to see you on TV.